Irish Verse
An Anthology

DOVER · THRIFT · EDITIONS

Irish Verse
An Anthology

EDITED BY
BOB BLAISDELL

DOVER PUBLICATIONS, INC.
Mineola, New York

DOVER THRIFT EDITIONS

GENERAL EDITOR: PAUL NEGRI
EDITOR OF THIS VOLUME: BOB BLAISDELL

ACKNOWLEDGMENTS: see page vii

Copyright

Copyright © 2002 by Dover Publications, Inc.
All rights reserved under Pan American and International Copyright Conventions.

Published in Canada by General Publishing Company, Ltd., 895 Don Mills Road,
400-2 Park Centre, Toronto, Ontario M3C 1W3.
Published in the United Kingdom by David & Charles, Brunel House, Forde Close,
Newton Abbot, Devon, TQ12 4PU.

Bibliographical Note

Irish Verse: An Anthology, first published in 2002, is a new selection of Irish poetry
reprinted from standard texts.

Library of Congress Cataloging-in-Publication Data

Irish verse : an anthology / edited by Bob Blaisdell.
    p. cm.
  ISBN 0-486-41914-2 (pbk.)
    1. Irish poetry—Translations into English. 2. Ireland—Poetry. I. Blaisdell, Robert.

PB1424 .I75 2002
891.6'21008—dc21

2001047764

Manufactured in the United States of America
Dover Publications, Inc., 31 East 2nd Street, Mineola, N.Y. 11501

Note

An island at the northwestern edge of the world, free of Roman dominance and for the most part of Roman influence, met up with Christianity in the sixth century. Over the next two centuries, through its own oral literature and scholarly Christian traditions, it created the first recorded literature of western Europe. This period represents the time "when Ireland was the school of the west, the quiet habitation of sanctity and literature," noted Samuel Johnson. The early Christians had found an easy and independent home, free of most of the travails of Roman Europe. Monks who devoted their lives to study and contemplation recorded and wrote poetry, as well as trained students from other parts of Europe. In spite of Anglo-Saxon intrusions and influxes that began in the twelfth century, Irish flourished as the common and literary language. In bardic schools from the twelfth to the seventeenth centuries, young men born to the profession learned Irish literature and composed their poems in dark, silent cells—as was the custom—before sharing their songs as they wandered the countryside. This effective and folkish dissemination of Irish literature, however, began to disappear by the early nineteenth century, when the Catholic Church decided that in its schools Irish children would be taught only in English. And then, with the devastating famines of 1846 and 1847 that scattered millions of the surviving population through emigration, the Irish language was nearly obliterated. At the end of the nineteenth and the beginning of the twentieth century, poetry and patriotism helped revive the Irish language which today, in the beginning of the twenty-first century, is becoming the language of choice for many contemporary Irish writers.

More than a third of the poems featured in this anthology are translations from Ireland's literature in Irish; and though none of its ancient (and often anonymous) writers have earned the fame of Ireland's poets, e.g., Jonathan Swift, Oscar Wilde, John Millington Synge, or William Butler Yeats, their poems may strike us as even more immediately engaging. For instance, from the tenth century "On the Flightiness of Thought," the anonymous monk and poet begins: "Shame to my thoughts, how they stray from me! / I fear great danger from it on the day of eternal Doom." And he follows with a list of such strayings, despairing, "Though one should try to bind them or put shackles on their feet, / They are neither constant nor mindful to take a spell of rest. / Neither sword-edge nor crack of whip will keep them down strongly: / As slippery as an eel's tail they glide out of my grasp."[1]

Ancient Irish poetry reveals the personal drama and interest in nature that today's readers may have thought of as a wholly modern or a mostly Eastern development: "A hedge of trees surrounds me," writes the ancient scribe, "A blackbird's lay sings to me; / Above my lined booklet / The trilling birds chant to me. / In a grey mantle from the top of bushes / The cuckoo sings: / Verily—may the Lord shield me!—/ Well do I write under the greenwood."[2] The scholar and translator Kuno Meyer comments: "It is characteristic of these poems that in none of them do we get an elaborate or sustained description of any scene or scenery, but rather a succession of pictures and images which the poet, like the impressionist, calls up before us by light and skilful touches. Like the Japanese, the Celts were always quick to take an artistic hint; they avoid the obvious and the commonplace; the half-said thing to them is dearest."[3] The ancient poems are not folkish, cheery or political: they are poems as individual and personal as, for instance, the great poems Yeats wrote a thousand years later. There are so many gorgeous and not nearly famous enough ancient lyrics that an anthology of a hundred and twelve poems cannot contain enough of them. Fortunately, an abundance of studies and translations of ancient Irish poetry are readily available.

"Ireland is a country that has two literatures—one a literature in Irish—Gaelic literature—that has been cultivated continuously since the eighth century, and the other a literature in English—Anglo-Irish literature—that took its rise in the eighteenth century," writes the poet Padraic Colum.[4] It was in the beginning of the eighteenth century that Jonathan Swift, a Protestant, who in many ways did not sympathize with most of Ireland's people or culture, became the most famous and important Irish writer of the century. Through his essays and satires, he became a spokesman for Irish causes and regularly attacked English prejudices and injustices. As a poet, his wit and ear for the colloquial speech of English-speaking Dublin give us everyday impressions of his world as, for instance, in the voices of market-women: "Be not sparing / Leave off swearing: / Buy my herring / Fresh from Malahide, / Better ne'er was tried. / Come eat 'em with pure fresh butter and mustard, / Their bellies are soft, and as white as a custard. / Come, sixpence a dozen to get me some bread, / Or, like my own herrings, I soon shall be dead."[5]

1. See page 11 for the entire poem.
2. "The Scribe: 'A Hedge of Trees'," page 1.
3. Kuno Meyer. *Ancient Irish Lyrics*. London. 1913. xiii.
4. Padraic Colum. *Anthology of Irish Verse*. New York. 1922.
5. From the series "Verses Made for Women Who Cry Apples, etc." pages 58–60.

Simultaneous with the growing pervasiveness of English and the extinguishing of Irish came a scholarly interest in the native Irish literature and a flourishing of translation. In the nineteenth century, folk songs and lyrics made their way into English through such outstanding scholars as William Ferguson, James Clarence Mangan, Alfred Perceval Graves, Eleanor Hull, and Douglas Hyde. (In 1893, Hyde lamented, however, "If these old songs had been collected a hundred or a hundred and fifty years ago, together with the stories that belong to them . . . they would make the most valuable and interesting store and treasure amongst the nations that speak a Celtic language. . . . Alas! it is an incredible loss."[6]) As a young man, Yeats discovered his own voice and power through his reading of such translations, editing anthologies of Irish literature and learning Irish himself. His early "Down by the Salley Gardens" is reminiscent of the folk songs he admired. ("Down by the salley gardens my love and I did meet; / She passed the salley gardens with little snow-white feet. / She bid me take love easy, as the leaves grow on the tree; / But I, being young and foolish, with her would not agree."[7])

By most accounts, the creative surge of Irish literature in English in the first decade of the twentieth century owes much to the writers' awareness of the distinctive forms and rhythms of Irish. "What is really important about verse forms," writes Frank O'Connor, "is not so much that they should be Irish as that they should not be English. Merely because the similarity of language always threatens to suck the writer into forms of the more highly evolved literature, he has to adopt every device to keep his distance from it."[8] The revival of Irish helped spur not only Ireland's independence in 1923 but its remarkable literary showing in the twentieth century, from Yeats, Synge, and James Joyce to O'Connor himself, Seamas Heaney, and William Trevor, among many others.

Fourteen hundred years of poetry by writers of vastly different backgrounds, interests, and beliefs cannot be summed up by any all-encompassing terms. I have attempted to include poems of Irish or Anglo-Irish origin that seem exceptionally fine and—for the casual reader with little or no background in the history of Ireland—easily comprehensible. I have arranged the poems in a chronological fashion, with the author's year of birth (when known) determining the poem's placement. The dates I have provided for the ancient and anonymous poems are *approximate*, derived from the guesses of scholars and previous editors. It is helpful to remember that the wonderful and usually anonymous street songs and ballads of the eighteenth and nineteenth centuries were usually in the air for some time before being written down. Furthermore, many of the folk songs

---

6. Douglas Hyde. *Abhrain Gradh Chuige Connacht or Love Songs of Connaught.* London. 1893. 65.
7. "Down by the Salley Gardens," p. 103.
8. Frank O'Connor. *A Short History of Irish Literature: A Backward Look.* New York. 1967.

developed in many different versions from region to region over genera-
tions before being translated by singers or scholars. Almost all of the
poems, which date from the seventh century to 1922, have appeared in
earlier anthologies, most notably Kuno Meyer's *Ancient Irish Lyrics* (1913),
Padraic Colum's *Anthology of Irish Verse* (1922), Eleanor Hull's *The Poem-
Book of the Gael* (1913), Alfred Perceval Graves' *The Book of Irish Poetry*
(1915), H. Halliday Sparling's *Irish Minstrelsy* (Third Edition, 1893), and
John Cooke's *The Dublin Book of Irish Verse* (1909). For those readers in-
terested in further literary and historical background, I suggest Frank
O'Connor's delightful *A Short History of Irish Literature: A Backward Look*.

Other books consulted but not noted above include *A Literary History
of Ireland*, Douglas Hyde (1906); *The Oxford Companion to Irish
Literature*, Robert Welch and Bruce Stewart (1996); *An Anthology of Irish
Literature*, David H. Greene (1954); *1000 Years of Irish Poetry*, Kathleen
Hoagland (1947); *The New Oxford Book of Irish Verse*, Thomas Kinsella
(1986); *A Golden Treasury of Irish Poetry*: A.D. 600–1200, David Greene
and Frank O'Connor; *Kings, Lords, & Commons: An Anthology from the
Irish*, Frank O'Connor; *Text Book of Irish Literature*, Eleanor Hull (1908);
Literature in Ireland, Thomas MacDonagh (1916); *Irish Poets of To-Day*,
L. D'O. Walters (1921); *The New Spirit of "The Nation,"* Martin Mac-
Dermott (1894); and *The Poetical Works of Jonathan Swift* (1806).

—Bob Blaisdell

Acknowledgments

Padraic Colum: "An Old Woman of the Roads" from *The Dublin Book of Irish Verse, 1728–1909* (edited by John Cooke), Dublin and London, 1909. Reprinted with the kind permission of Maire Colum O'Sullivan.

Francis A. Fahy: "Little Mary Cassidy" from *The Book of Irish Poetry* (edited by Alfred Perceval Graves), Frederick A. Stokes Company, New York, 1915. Reprinted with the kind permission of the Francis Fahy Society (www.kinvara.com/francisfahy).

Alfred Perceval Graves: "The Song of the Ghost" from *Anthology of Irish Verse* (edited by Padraic Colum), Boni and Liveright, New York, 1922; "The Irish Spinning-Wheel" from *The Dublin Book of Irish Verse, 1728–1909* (edited by John Cooke), Dublin and London, 1909. Both poems are reprinted with the kind permission of Richard Perceval Graves.

James Stephens: "In the Poppy Field" from *Irish Poets of To-Day, An Anthology* (compiled by L. D'O. Walters), T. Fisher Unwin Ltd., London, 1921; "The Whisperer" and "The Shell" from *The Dublin Book of Irish Verse, 1728–1909* (edited by John Cooke), Dublin and London, 1909. All are reprinted with the kind permission of The Society of Authors as the Literary Representative of the Estate of James Stephens.

William Butler Yeats: "Down by the Salley Gardens" from Yeats' *Crossways* (1889) as published in *Poems* by Unwin, London, 1895; "The Ballad of Father Gilligan" and "To Ireland in the Coming Times" from Yeats' *Rose* (1893) as published in *Poems* by Unwin, London, 1895; "The Host of the Air" and "The Song of Wandering Aengus" from Yeats' *The Wind Among the Reeds* (second edition) as published by Elkin Mathews, London, 1899; "September 1913" from Yeats' *Responsibilities: Poems and a Play* as published by The Cuala Press, Churchtown, Dundrum, 1914; "In Memory of Major Robert Gregory" and "An Irish Airman Foresees His Death" from Yeats' *The Wild Swans at Coole* (1919) as published in *Later Poems* by Macmillan and Co., London, 1922; "Easter 1916" and "The Second Coming" from Yeats' *Michael Robartes and the Dancer* (1921) as published in *Later Poems* by Macmillan and Co., London, 1922. All are reprinted with the kind permission of A. P. Watt Ltd. on behalf of Michael B. Yeats.

Contents

III. *Poetry in English Since Swift*   57

Irish Verse

An Anthology

I. *Poems from the Irish*

ANONYMOUS

The Scribe: "A Hedge of Trees"
This is a pair of ancient Irish quatrains, circa seventh century.

A hedge of trees surrounds me,
A blackbird's lay sings to me;
Above my lined booklet
The trilling birds chant to me.

In a grey mantle from the top of bushes
The cuckoo sings:
Verily—may the Lord shield me!—
Well do I write under the greenwood.

—translated by Kuno Meyer

The Blackbird
*This poem was written by a monk in the margin of a book
he was copying, circa seventh century.*

Ah, blackbird, thou art satisfied
Where thy nest is in the bush:
Hermit that clinkest no bell,
Sweet, soft, peaceful is thy note.

—translated by Kuno Meyer

1

The Feìlire of Adamnan

Though ascribed to St. Adamnan, Abbot of Iona (died 704),
the biographer of St. Columba, the ancient Irish litany, judg-
ing by its languages, is later. (Note by Alfred Perceval Graves)

Saints of Four Seasons!
Saints of the Year!
Loving, I pray to you; longing, I say to you:
Save me from angers, dreeings, and dangers!
Saints of Four Seasons!
Saints of the Year!

Saints of Green Springtime!
Saints of the Year!
Patraic and Grighair, Brighid be near!
My last breath gather with God's Foster Father!
Saints of Green Springtime!
Saints of the Year!

Saints of Gold Summer!
Saints of the Year!
(Poesy wingeth me! Fancy far bringeth me!)
Guide ye me on to Mary's Sweet Son!
Saints of Gold Summer!
Saints of the Year!

Saints of Red Autumn!
Saints of the Year!
Lo! I am cheery! Michil and Mary
Open wide Heaven to my soul bereaven!
Saints of Red Autumn!
Saints of the Year!

Saints of Grey Winter!
Saints of the Year!
Outside God's Palace fiends wait in malice—
Let them not win my soul going in!
Saints of Grey Winter!
Saints of the Year!

Saints of Four Seasons!
Saints of the Year!
Waking or sleeping, to my grave creeping,
Life in its Night, hold me God's light!
Saints of Four Seasons!
Saints of the Year!

—translated by Patrick J. McCall

St. Patrick's Breastplate

*"According to tradition," writes Padraic Colum, "St. Patrick uttered it
while on his way to Tara, where he was for the first time to confront
the power of the Pagan High-King of Ireland. Assassins were in wait
for him and his companions, but as he chanted the hymn it seemed
to the hidden band that a herd of deer went by," circa eighth century.*

I arise today
Through the strength of heaven:
Light of sun,
Radiance of moon,
Splendour of fire,
Speed of lightning,
Swiftness of wind,
Depth of sea,
Stability of earth,
Firmness of rock.

I arise today
Through God's strength to pilot me:
God's might to uphold me,
God's wisdom to guide me,
God's eye to look before me,
God's ear to hear me,
God's word to speak for me,
God's hand to guard me,
God's way to lie before me,
God's shield to protect me,
God's host to save me
From snares of devils,
From temptations of vices,
From every one who shall wish me ill,
Afar and anear,
Alone and in a multitude.

Christ to shield me today
Against poison, against burning,
Against drowning, against wounding,
So that there may come to me abundance of reward.
Christ with me, Christ before me, Christ behind me,
Christ in me, Christ beneath me, Christ above me,
Christ on my right, Christ on my left,
Christ when I lie down, Christ when I sit down, Christ when I arise,
Christ in the heart of every man who thinks of me,
Christ in the mouth of every one who speaks of me,
Christ in every eye that sees me,
Christ in every ear that hears me.

I arise today
Through a mighty strength, the invocation of the Trinity,
Through belief in the threeness,
Through confession of the oneness
Of the Creator of Creation.

—translated by Kuno Meyer

The Student and His Cat

The Irish of this playful poem was written by a student of the Monastery of Carinthia on a copy of St. Paul's Epistles about the close of the eighth century. (Note by Eleanor Hull)

I and Pangur Bán, my cat,
'Tis a like task we are at;
Hunting mice is his delight,
Hunting words I sit all night.

Better far than praise of men
'Tis to sit with book and pen;
Pangur bears me no ill-will,
He, too, plies his simple skill.

'Tis a merry thing to see
At our tasks how glad are we,
When at home we sit and find
Entertainment to our mind.

Oftentimes a mouse will stray
In the hero Pangur's way;
Oftentimes my keen thought set
Takes a meaning in its net.

'Gainst the wall he sets his eye
Full and fierce and sharp and sly;
'Gainst the wall of knowledge I
All my little wisdom try.

When a mouse darts from its den,
O! how glad is Pangur then;
O! what gladness do I prove
When I solve the doubts I love.

So in peace our task we ply,
Pangur Bán, my cat, and I;
In our arts we find our bliss,
I have mine, and he has his.

Practice every day has made
Pangur perfect in his trade;
I get wisdom day and night,
Turning darkness into light.

—translated by Robin Flower

Summer Has Come
(circa ninth century)

Summer has come, healthy and free,
Whence the brown wood is bent to the ground:
The slender nimble deer leap,
And the path of seals is smooth.

The cuckoo sings gentle music,
Whence there is smooth peaceful calm:
Gentle birds skip upon the hill,
And swift grey stags.

Heat has laid hold of the rest of the deer—
The lovely cry of curly packs!
The white extent of the strand smiles,
There the swift sea is roused.

A sound of playful breezes in the tops
Of a black oakwood is Drum Daill,
The noble hornless herd runs,
To whom Cuan-wood is a shelter.

Green bursts out on every herb,
The top of the green oakwood is bushy,
Summer has come, winter has gone,
Twisted hollies wound the hound.

The blackbird sings a loud strain,
To him the live wood is a heritage,
The sad angry sea is fallen asleep,
The speckled salmon leaps.

The sun smiles over every land,—
A parting for me from the brood of cares:
Hounds bark, stags tryst,
Ravens flourish, summer has come!

—translated by Kuno Meyer

The Sacred Trinity

*The Irish had a passion for triads. Here, in an ancient, circa
ninth century verse, the triad is put to use to prove the Trinity.*

Three folds of the cloth, yet one only napkin is there,
Three joints in the finger, but still only one finger fair;
Three leaves of the shamrock, yet no more than one shamrock to wear.
Frost, snow-flakes and ice, all in water their origin share,
Three Persons in God; to one God alone we make prayer.

—*translated by Eleanor Hull*

Early Irish Triads

From the ninth century collection of that name.

Three slender ones whereon the whole Earth swings:
The thin milk stream that in the keeler sings,
The thin green blade that from the cornfield springs,
The thin grey thread the housewife's shuttle flings.

Three finenesses that foulness keep from sight:
Fine manners in the most misfeatured wight,
Fine shapes of art by servile fingers moulded,
Fine wisdom from a hunch-back's brain unfolded.

Three fewnesses that better are than plenty:
A fewness of fine words—but one in twenty—
A fewness of milch-cows, when grass is shrinking;
Fewness of friends when beer is best for drinking.

Three graceless sisters in the bond of unity
Are lightness, flightiness and importunity.

Three clouds, the most obscuring Wisdom's glance:
Forgetfulness, half-knowledge, ignorance.

Three signs of ill-bred folk in every nation:
A visit lengthened to a visitation,
Staring, and over-much interrogation.

Three keys that most unlock our secret thinking
Are love and trustfulness and over-drinking.

Three the receivers are of stolen goods:
A cloak, the cloak of night, the cloak of woods.

Three unions, each of peace a proved miscarriage:
Confederate feats, joint ploughland, bonds of marriage.

Three excellencies of our dress are these:
Elegance, durability and ease.

Three aged sisters, not too hard to guess,
Are groaning, chastity and ugliness.

Three glories of a gathering free from strife:
Swift hound, proud steed and beautiful young wife.

The world's three laughing stocks (be warned and wiser!):
An angry man, a jealous and a miser.

Three powers advantaging a Chieftain most
Are Peace and Justice and an armed host.
Three worst of snares upon a Chieftain's way:
Sloth, treachery and evil counsel they!

Three ruins of a tribe to west or east:
A lying Chief, false Brehon, lustful Priest.

The rudest three of all the sons of earth:
A youngster of an old man making mirth,
A strong man at a sick man poking fun,
A wise man gibing at a foolish one.

Three signs that show a fop; the comb-track in his hair,
The track of his nice teeth upon his nibbled fare,
His cane track in the dust, oft as he takes the air.

Three sparks that light the fire of love are these:
Glamour of face, and grace, and speech of ease.

Three steadinesses of wise womanhood:
A steady tongue, through evil as through good;
A steady chastity, whoso else shall stray;
Steady house-service, all and every day.

Three signs of increase: kine that low,
When milk unto their calves they owe;
The hammer on the anvil's brow,
The pleasant swishing of the plough.

Three sisters false: I would! I might! I may!
Three timorous brothers: Hearken! Hush! and Stay!

Three coffers of a depth unknown
Are His who occupies the throne,
The Church's, and the privileged Poet's own.

—*translated by Alfred Perceval Graves*

The Song of Manchan the Hermit

The subject was Abbot of Liath Manchan, now Lemanaghan, in King's County. He died 665 A.D. The verse was composed circa ninth century.

I wish, O Son of the Living God, O Ancient Eternal King,
For a hidden hut in the wilderness, a simple secluded thing.

The all-blithe lithe little lark in his place, chanting his lightsome lay;
The calm, clear pool of the Spirit's grace, washing my sins away.

A wide, wild woodland on every side, its shades the nursery
Of glad-voiced songsters, who at day-dawn chant their sweet psalm for me.

A southern aspect to catch the sun, a brook across the floor,
A choice land, rich with gracious gifts, down-stretching from my door.

Few men and wise, these I would prize, men of content and power,
To raise Thy praise throughout the days at each canonical hour.

Four times three, three times four, fitted for every need,
To the King of the Sun praying each one, this were a grace, indeed.

Twelve in the church to chant the hours, kneeling there twain and twain;
And I before, near the chancel door, listening their low refrain.

A pleasant church with an Altar-cloth, where Christ sits at the board,
And a shining candle shedding its ray on the white words of the Lord.

Brief meals between, when prayer is done, our modest needs supply;
No greed in our share of the simple fare, no boasting or ribaldry.

This is the husbandry I choose, laborious, simple, free,
The fragrant leek about my door, the hen and the humble bee.

Rough raiment of tweed, enough for my need, this will my King allow;
And I to be sitting praying to God under every leafy bough.

—translated by Eleanor Hull

The Old Woman of Beare

(circa ninth century)

Ebbtide to me!
My life drifts downward with the drifting sea;
Old age has caught and compassed me about,
The tides of time run out.

The "Hag of Beare!"
'Tis thus I hear the young girls jeer and mock;
Yet I, who in these cast-off clouts appear,
Once donned a queenly smock.

Ye love but self,
Ye churls! today ye worship pelf!
But in the days I lived we sought for men,
We loved our lovers then!

Ah! swiftly when
Their splendid chariots coursed upon the plain,
I checked their pace, for me they flew amain,
Held in by curb and rein.

I envy not the old,
Whom gold adorns, whom richest robes enfold,
But ah! the girls, who pass my cell at morn,
While I am shorn!

On sweet May-morn
Their ringing laughter on the breeze is borne,
While I, who shake with ague and with age,
In Litanies engage.

Amen! and woe is me!
I lie here rotting like a broken tree;
Each acorn has its day and needs must fall,
Time makes an end of all!

I had my day with kings!
We drank the brimming mead, the ruddy wine,
Where now I drink whey-water; for company more fine
Than shrivelled hags, hag though I am, I pine.

The flood-tide thine!
Mine but the low down-curling ebb-tide's flow,
My youth, my hope, are carried from my hand,
Thy flood-tide foams to land.

My body drops
Slowly but sure towards the abode we know;
When God's High Son takes from me all my props
It will be time to go!

Bony my arms and bare
Could you but see them 'neath the mantle's flap.
Wizened and worn, that once were round and fair,
When kings lay in my lap.

'Tis, "O my God" with me,
Many prayers said, yet more prayers left undone;
If I could spread my garment in the sun
I'd say them, every one.

The sea-wave talks,
Athwart the frozen earth grim winter stalks;
Young Fermod, son of Mugh, ne'er said me nay,
Yet he comes not today.

How still they row,
Oar dipped by oar the wavering reeds among,
To Alma's shore they press, a ghostly throng,
Deeply they sleep and long.

No lightsome laugh
Disturbs my fireside's stillness; shadows fall,
And quiet forms are gathering round my hearth,
Yet lies the hand of silence on them all.

I do not deem it ill
That a nun's veil should rest upon my head;
But finer far my feast-robe's various hue
To me, when all is said.

My very cloak grows old;
Grey is its tint, its woof is frayed and thin;
I seem to feel grey hairs within its fold,
Or are they on my skin?

O happy Isle of Ocean,
Thy flood-tide leaps to meet the eddying wave
Lifting it up and onward. Till the grave
The sea-wave comes not after ebb for me.

I find them not
Those sunny sands I knew so well of yore;
Only the surf's sad roar sounds up to me,
My tide will turn no more.

—translated by Eleanor Hull

In Praise of May

Ascribed to Fionn mac Cumhaill, circa third century, who, it is said, was inspired to write the poem after eating of the "Salmon of Knowledge" at the River Boyne. The poem was probably written circa ninth–tenth century.

May-day! delightful day!
Bright colours play the vale along.
Now wakes at morning's slender ray
Wild and gay the blackbird's song.

Now comes the bird of dusty hue,
The loud cuckoo, the summer-lover;
Branchy trees are thick with leaves;
The bitter, evil time is over.

Swift horses gather nigh
Where half dry the river goes;
Tufted heather clothes the height;
Weak and white the bogdown blows.

Corncrake sings from eve to morn,
Deep in corn, a strenuous bard!
Sings the virgin waterfall,
White and tall, her one sweet word.

Loaded bees with puny power
Goodly flower-harvest win;
Cattle roam with muddy flanks;
Busy ants go out and in.

Through the wild harp of the wood
Making music roars the gale—
Now it settles without motion,
On the ocean sleeps the sail.

Men grow mighty in the May,
Proud and gay the maidens grow;
Fair is every wooded height;
Fair and bright the plain below.

A bright shaft has smit the streams,
With gold gleams the water-flag;
Leaps the fish, and on the hills
Ardour thrills the leaping stag.

Loudly carols the lark on high,
Small and shy, his tireless lay,
Singing in wildest, merriest mood,
Delicate-hued, delightful May.

—translated by T. W. Rolleston

On the Flightiness of Thought
(circa tenth century)

Shame to my thoughts, how they stray from me!
I fear great danger from it on the day of eternal Doom.

During the psalms they wander on a path that is not right:
They fash, they fret, they misbehave before the eyes of great God.

Through eager crowds, through companies of wanton women,
Through woods, through cities—swifter they are than the wind.

Now through paths of loveliness, anon of riotous shame!

Without a ferry or ever missing a step they go across every sea:
Swiftly they leap in one bound from earth to heaven.

They run a race of folly anear and afar:
After a course of giddiness they return to their home.

Though one should try to bind them or put shackles on their feet,
They are neither constant nor mindful to take a spell of rest.

Neither sword-edge nor crack of whip will keep them down strongly:
As slippery as an eel's tail they glide out of my grasp.

Neither lock nor firm-vaulted dungeon nor any fetter on earth,
Stronghold nor sea nor bleak fastness restrains them from their course.

O beloved truly chaste Christ to whom every eye is clear,
May the grace of the seven-fold Spirit come to keep them, to check them!

Rule this heart of mine, O dread God of the elements,
That Thou mayst be my love, that I may do Thy will.

That I may reach Christ with His chosen companions, that we may be
    together!
They are neither fickle nor inconstant—not as *I* am.

—translated by Kuno Meyer

A Song of Winter
(circa tenth century)

Cold, cold!
Cold tonight is broad Moylurg,
Higher the snow than the mountain-range,
The deer cannot get at their food.

Cold till Doom!
The storm has spread over all:
A river is each furrow upon the slope,
Each ford a full pool.

A great tidal sea is each loch,
A full loch is each pool:
Horses cannot get over the ford of Ross,
No more can two feet get there.

The fish of Ireland are a-roaming,
There is no strand which the wave does not pound,
Not a town there is in the land,
Not a bell is heard, no crane talks.

The wolves of Cuan-wood get
Neither rest nor sleep in their lair,
The little wren cannot find
Shelter in her nest on the slope of Lon.

Keen wind and cold ice
Has burst upon the little company of birds,
The blackbird cannot get a lee to her liking,
Shelter for its side in Cuan-wood.

Cosy our pot on its hook,
Crazy the hut on the slope of Lon:
The snow has crushed the wood here,
Toilsome to climb up Ben-bo.

Glenn Rye's ancient bird
From the bitter wind gets grief;
Great her misery and her pain,
The ice will get into her mouth.

From flock and from down to rise—
Take it to heart!—were folly for thee:
Ice in heaps on every ford—
That is why I say 'cold'!

—translated by Kuno Meyer

King and Hermit

Marvan, brother of King Gooary of Connaught in the seventh century, had re-nounced the life of a warrior-prince for that of a hermit. The king endeavoured to persuade his brother to return to his court, when the following colloquy took place between them. (Note by Kuno Meyer; the poem was composed circa tenth century)

GOOARY
Why, hermit Marvan, sleepest thou not
Upon a feather quilt?
Why rather sleepest thou abroad
Upon a pitchpine floor?

MARVAN

I have a shieling in the wood,
None knows it save my God:
An ash-tree on the hither side, a hazel-bush beyond,
A huge old tree encompasses it.

Two heath-clad doorposts for support,
And a lintel of honeysuckle:
The forest around its narrowness sheds
Its mast upon fat swine.

The size of my shieling tiny, not too tiny,
Many are its familiar paths:
From its gable a sweet strain sings
A she-bird in her cloak of the ousel's hue.

The stags of Oakridge leap
Into the river of clear banks:
Thence red Roiny can be seen,
Glorious Muckraw and Moinmoy.*

A hiding mane of green-barked yew
Supports the sky:
Beautiful spot! the large green of an oak
Fronting the storm.

A tree of apples—great its bounty!
Like a hostel, vast!
A pretty bush, thick as a fist, of tiny hazel-nuts,
A green mass of branches.

A choice pure spring and princely water
To drink:
There spring watercresses, yew-berries,
Ivy-bushes thick as a man.

Around it tame swine lie down,
Goats, pigs,
Wild swine, grazing deer,
A badger's brood.

A peaceful troop, a heavy host of denizens of the soil,
A-trysting at my house:
To meet them foxes come,
How delightful!

Fairest princes come to my house,
A ready gathering:

*Names of well-known plains.—*Meyer.*

Pure water, perennial bushes,
Salmon, trout.

A bush of rowan, black sloes,
Dusky blackthorns,
Plenty of food, acorns, pure berries,
Bare flags.

A clutch of eggs, honey, delicious mast,
God has sent it:
Sweet apples, red whortleberries,
And blaeberries.

Ale with herbs, a dish of strawberries
Of good taste and colour,
Haws, berries of the juniper,
Sloes, nuts.

A cup with mead of hazel-nut, blue-bells,
Quick-growing rushes,
Dun oaklets, manes of briar,
Goodly sweet tangle.

When brilliant summer-time spreads its coloured mantle,
Sweet-tasting fragrance!
Pignuts, wild marjoram, green leeks,
Verdant pureness!

The music of the bright red-breasted men,
A lovely movement!
The strain of the thrush, familiar cuckoos
Above my house.

Swarms of bees and chafers, the little musicians of the world,
A gentle chorus:
Wild geese and ducks, shortly before summer's end,
The music of the dark torrent.

An active songster, a lively wren
From the hazel-bough,
Beautiful hooded birds, woodpeckers,
A vast multitude!

Fair white birds come, herons, seagulls,
The cuckoo sings between—
No mournful music! dun heathpoults
Out of the russet heather.

The lowing of heifers in summer,
Brightest of seasons!

Not bitter, toilsome over the fertile plain,
Delightful, smooth!

The voice of the wind against the branchy wood
Upon the deep-blue sky:
Falls of the river, the note of the swan,
Delicious music!

The bravest band make cheer to me,
Who have not been hired:
In the eyes of Christ the ever-young I am no worse off
Than thou art.

Though thou rejoicest in thy own pleasures,
Greater than any wealth;
I am grateful for what is given me
From my good Christ.

Without an hour of fighting, without the din of strife
In my house,
Grateful to the Prince who giveth every good
To me in my shieling.

GOOARY

I would give my glorious kingship
With the share of my father's heritage—
To the hour of my death I would forfeit it
To be in thy company, my Marvan.

—translated by Kuno Meyer

The Scribe: "For Weariness My Hand Writes Ill"

This poem is ascribed to St. Columba (b. 521,
d. 597), but written circa eleventh century.

For weariness my hand writes ill,
    My small, sharp quill runs rough and slow;
Its slender beak with failing craft
    Puts forth its draught of dark, blue flow.

And yet God's blessed wisdom gleams
    And streams beneath my fair-brown palm
The while quick jets of holly ink
    The letters link of prayer or psalm.

So, still my dripping pen is fain
    To cross the plain of parchment white,
Unceasing at some rich man's call,
    Till wearied all am I tonight.

—translated by Alfred Perceval Graves

The Deserted Home
(circa eleventh century)

Sadly talks the blackbird here.
Well I know the woe he found:
No matter who cut down his nest,
For its young it was destroyed.

I myself not long ago
Found the woe he now has found.
Well I read thy song, O bird,
For the ruin of thy home.

Thy heart, O blackbird, burnt within
At the deed of reckless man:
Thy nest bereft of young and egg
The cowherd deems a trifling tale.

At thy clear notes they used to come,
Thy new-fledged children, from afar;
No bird now comes from out thy house,
Across its edge the nettle grows.

They murdered them, the cowherd lads,
All thy children in one day:
One the fate to me and thee,
My own children live no more.

There was feeding by thy side
Thy mate, a bird from o'er the sea:
Then the snare entangled her,
At the cowherds' hands she died.

O Thou, the Shaper of the world!
Uneven hands Thou layst on us:
Our fellows at our side are spared,
Their wives and children are alive.

A fairy host came as a blast
To bring destruction to our house:
Though bloodless was their taking off,
Yet dire as slaughter by the sword.

Woe for our wife, woe for our young!
The sadness of our grief is great:
No trace of them within, without—
And therefore is my heart so sad.

—translated by Kuno Meyer

Colum Cille's Greeting to Ireland

*This poem was ascribed to Saint Columba (b. 521,
d. 597), but was probably written circa twelfth century.*

Delightful to be on the Hill of Howth
Before going over the white-haired sea:
The dashing of the wave against its face,
The bareness of its shores and of its border.

Delightful to be on the Hill of Howth
After coming over the white-bosomed sea;
To be rowing one's little coracle,
Ochone! on the wild-waved shore.

Great is the speed of my coracle,
And its stern turned upon Derry:
Grievous is my errand over the main,
Travelling to Alba of the beetling brows.

My foot in my tuneful coracle,
My sad heart tearful:
A man without guidance is weak,
Blind are all the ignorant.

There is a grey eye
That will look back upon Erin:
It shall never see again
The men of Erin nor her women.

I stretch my glance across the brine
From the firm oaken planks:
Many are the tears of my bright soft grey eye
As I look back upon Erin.

My mind is upon Erin,
Upon Loch Lene, upon Linny,

Upon the land where Ulstermen are,
Upon gentle Munster and upon Meath.

Many in the East are lanky chiels,
Many diseases there and distempers,
Many they with scanty dress,
Many the hard and jealous hearts.

Plentiful in the West the fruit of the apple-tree,
Many kings and princes;
Plentiful are luxurious sloes,
Plentiful oak-woods of noble mast.

Melodious her clerics, melodious her birds,
Gentle her youths, wise her elders,
Illustrious her men, famous to behold,
Illustrious her women for fond espousal.

It is in the West sweet Brendan is,
And Colum son of Criffan,
And in the West fair Baithin shall be,
And in the West shall be Adamnan.

Carry my greeting after that
To Comgall of eternal life:
Carry my greeting after that
To the stately king of fair Navan.

Carry with thee, thou fair youth,
My blessing and my benediction:
One half upon Erin, sevenfold,
And half upon Alba at the same time.

Carry my blessing with thee to the West,
My heart is broken in my breast:
Should sudden death overtake me,
It is for my great love of the Gael.

Gael! Gael! beloved name!
It gladdens the heart to invoke it:
Beloved is Cummin of the beauteous hair,
Beloved are Cainnech and Comgall.

Were all Alba mine
From its centre to its border,
I would rather have the site of a house
In the middle of fair Derry.

It is for this I love Derry,
For its smoothness, for its purity,

And for its crowd of white angels
From one end to another.

It is for this I love Derry,
For its smoothness, for its purity;
All full of angels
Is every leaf on the oaks of Derry.

My Derry, my little oak-grove,
My dwelling and my little cell,
O living God that art in Heaven above,
Woe to him who violates it!

Beloved are Durrow and Derry,
Beloved is Raphoe with purity,
Beloved Drumhome with its sweet acorns,
Beloved are Swords and Kells!

Beloved also to my heart in the West
Drumcliff on Culcinne's strand:
To gaze upon fair Loch Foyle—
The shape of its shores is delightful.

Delightful it is,
The deep-red ocean where the sea-gulls cry,
As I come from Derry afar,
It is peaceful and it is delightful.

—translated by Kuno Meyer

The Vision of Mac Conglinne
(circa twelfth century)

A vision that appeared to me,
An apparition wonderful
        I tell to all:
There was a coracle all of lard
Within a port of New-milk Lake
        Upon the world's smooth sea.

We went into that man-of-war,
'Twas warrior-like to take the road
        O'er ocean's heaving waves.
Our oar-strokes then we pulled
Across the level of the main,
Throwing the sea's harvest up
        Like honey, the sea-soil.

The fort we reached was beautiful,
With works of custards thick,
    Beyond the lake.
Fresh butter was the bridge in front,
The rubble dyke was fair white wheat,
    Bacon the palisade.

Stately, pleasantly it sat,
A compact house and strong.
    Then I went in:
The door of it was hung beef,
The threshold was dry bread,
    Cheese-curds the walls.

Smooth pillars of old cheese
And sappy bacon props
    Alternate ranged;
Stately beams of mellow cream,
White posts of real curds
    Kept up the house.

Behind it was a well of wine,
Beer and bragget in streams,
    Each full pool to the taste,
Malt in smooth wavy sea
Over a lard-spring's brink
    Flowed through the floor.

A lake of juicy pottage
Under a cream of oozy lard
    Lay 'twixt it and the sea.
Hedges of butter fenced it round,
Under a crest of white-mantled lard
    Around the wall outside.

A row of fragrant apple-trees,
An orchard in its pink-tipped bloom,
    Between it and the hill.
A forest tall of real leeks,
Of onions and of carrots, stood
    Behind the house.

Within, a household generous,
A welcome of red, firm-fed men,
    Around the fire:
Seven bead-strings and necklets seven
Of cheeses and of bits of tripe
    Round each man's neck.

The Chief in cloak of beefy fat
Beside his noble wife and fair
    I then beheld.
Below the lofty caldron's spit
Then the Dispenser I beheld,
    His fleshfork on his back.

Wheatlet son of Milklet,
Son of juicy Bacon,
    Is mine own name.
Honeyed Butter-roll
Is the man's name
    That bears my bag.

Haunch of Mutton
Is my dog's name,
    Of lovely leaps.
Lard, my wife,
Sweetly smiles
    Across the brose.

Cheese-curds, my daughter,
Goes round the spit,
    Fair is her fame.
Corned Beef is my son,
Who beams over a cloak,
    Enormous, of fat.

Savour of Savours
Is the name of my wife's maid:
Morning-early
Across New-milk Lake she went.

Beef-lard, my steed,
An excellent stallion
    That increases studs;
A guard against toil
Is the saddle of cheese
    Upon his back.

A large necklace of delicious cheese-curds
    Around his back;
His halter and his traces all
    Of fresh butter.

    —translated by Kuno Meyer

MURDOCH O'DALY (1180–1225)

The author, who was born in Connaught, was called Mur-
doch "the Scotchman" (Muredach Albanach), on account of
his affection for that country. (Note by Eleanor Hull)

Consecration

How great the tale, that there should be,
In God's Son's heart, a place for me!
That on a sinner's lips like mine,
The cross of Jesus Christ should shine!

Christ Jesus, bend me to Thy will,
My feet to urge, my griefs to still;
That even my flesh and blood may be
A temple sanctified to Thee.

No rest, no calm, my soul may win,
Because my body craves to sin,
Till Thou, dear Lord, Thyself impart
Peace to my head, light to my heart.

May consecration come from far,
Soft shining like the evening star!
My toilsome path make plain to me,
Until I come to rest in Thee.

—translated by Eleanor Hull

The Shaving of Murdoch

This poem was composed in the early thirteenth century, when Murdoch and
Cathal of the Red Hand, King of Connaught, entered the monastic life together.

Murdoch, whet thy knife, that we may shave our crowns to the Great
    King.
Let us sweetly give our vow, and the hair of both our heads to the Trinity.
I will shave mine to Mary, this is the doing of a true heart,
To Mary shave thou these locks, well-formed, soft-eyed man.
Seldom hast thou had, handsome man, a knife on thy hair to shave it,
Oftener has a sweet, soft queen, comb'd her hair beside thee.
Whenever it was that we did bathe, with Brian of the well-curled locks,
And once on a time that I did bathe, at the well of the fair-haired
    Boroimhe,
I strove in swimming with Ua Chais, on the cold waters of the Fergus.

When he came ashore from the stream, Ua Chais and I strove in a race.
These two knives, one to each, were given us by Duncan Cairbreach,
No knives of knives were better; shave gently then, Murdoch.
Whet your sword, Cathal, which wins the fertile Banva,
Ne'er was thy wrath heard without fighting, brave, red-handed Cathal,
Preserve our shaved heads from cold and from heat, gentle daughter of
 Joachim,
Preserve us in the land of heat, softest branch, Mary.

       —translated by Standish Hayes O'Grady

ANONYMOUS

Youth and Age

This poem is a selection by the translator from The Poem-Book
of Fionn, *a seventeenth-century collection of late medieval lyrics.*

 Once I was yellow-haired, and ringlets fell
  In clusters round my brow;
 Grizzled and sparse tonight my short grey crop,
  No lustre in it now.

 Better to me the shining locks of youth,
  Or raven's dusky hue,
 Than dear old age, which chilly wisdom brings,
  If what they say be true.

 I only know that as I pass the road
  No woman looks my way;
 They think my head and heart alike are cold—
  Yet I have had my day.

       —translated by Eleanor Hull

A Confession for Forgiveness
(circa late fifteenth–early sixteenth century)

  Outstretched on this bed,
   As if for the tomb,
  To make my confession,
   Lord, toward Thee I come!

  For all deeds of the flesh,
  Alas! ever fresh,
  Ill thoughts of the mind
  That my secret soul find;

For my eyes' lawless roving,
    My ears' lawless hearing,
My lips' lawless moving,
    My steps, sinward steering;

For everything spoken
    Or acted untrue;
For promises broken
    And broken anew;

For every one thing,
    In thought and in deed,
        In deed or in thought,
        Against Thy will wrought,
Oh, Heavenly King,
    For Thy pardon I plead!

—translated by Alfred Perceval Graves

Love Is a Mortal Disease
(circa early seventeenth century)

My grief and my pain! a mortal disease is love,
Woe, woe unto him who must prove it a month or even a day,
It hath broken my heart, and my bosom is burdened with sighs,
From dreaming of her gentle sleep hath forsaken mine eyes.

I met with the fairy host at the liss beside Ballyfinnane;
I asked them had they a herb for the curing of love's cruel pain.
They answered me softly and mildly, with many a pitying tone,
"When this torment comes into the heart it never goes out again."

It seems to me long till the tide washes up on the strand;
It seems to me long till the night shall fade into day;
It seems to me long till the cocks crow on every hand;
And rather than the world were I close beside my love.

Do not marry the grey old man, but marry the young man, dear;
Marry the lad who loves you, my grief, though he live not out the year;
Youthful you are, and kind, but your mind is not yet come to sense,
And if you live longer, the lads will be following you.

My woe and my plight! where tonight is the snowdrift and frost?
Or even I and my love together breasting the waves of the sea;
Without bark, without boat, without any vessel with me,
But I to be swimming, and my arm to be circling her waist!

—translated by Eleanor Hull

FEARFLATHA Ó GNÍMH (c. 1540–c. 1630)

The poet, who was born in Ulster, was known in English as O'Gnive, and was the bard of the O'Neill of Clandeboy.

The Downfall of the Gael
(circa 1612)

My heart is in woe,
    And my soul deep in trouble,—
For the mighty are low,
    And abased are the noble:

The Sons of the Gael
    Are in exile and mourning,
Worn, weary, and pale,
    As spent pilgrims returning;

Or men who, in flight
    From the field of disaster,
Beseech the black night
    On their flight to fall faster;

Or seamen aghast
    When their planks gape asunder,
And the waves fierce and fast
    Tumble through in hoarse thunder;

Or men whom we see
    That have got their death-omen—
Such wretches are we
    In the chains of our foemen!

Our courage is fear,
    Our nobility vileness,
Our hope is despair,
    And our comeliness foulness.

There is mist on our heads,
    And a cloud chill and hoary
Of black sorrow, sheds
    An eclipse on our glory.

From Boyne to the Linn
    Has the mandate been given,
That the children of Finn
    From their country be driven.

That the sons of the King—
   Oh, the treason and malice!—
Shall no more ride the ring
   In their own native valleys;

No more shall repair
   Where the hill foxes tarry,
Nor forth to the air
   Fling the hawk at her quarry:

For the plain shall be broke
   By the share of the stranger,
And the stone-mason's stroke
   Tell the woods of their danger;

The green hills and shore
   Be with white keeps disfigured,
And the Moat of Rathmore
   Be the Saxon churl's haggard!

The land of the lakes
   Shall no more know the prospect
Of valleys and brakes—
   So transform'd is her aspect!

The Gael cannot tell,
   In the uprooted wild-wood
And red ridgy dell,
   The old nurse of his childhood:

The nurse of his youth
   Is in doubt as she views him,
If the wan wretch, in truth,
   Be the child of her bosom.

We starve by the board,
   And we thirst amid wassail—
For the guest is the lord,
   And the host is the vassal!

Through the woods let us roam,
   Through the wastes wild and barren;
We are strangers at home!
   We are exiles in Erin!

And Erin's a bark
   O'er the wide waters driven!
And the tempest howls dark,
   And her side planks are riven!

And in billows of night
　　Swell the Saxon before her,—
Unite, oh, unite!
　　Or the billows burst o'er her!

　　　　　　　—*translated by Samuel Ferguson*

The Lament of O'Gnive

(early seventeenth century)

How dimm'd is the glory that circled the Gael,
And fall'n the high people of green Innisfail!
The sword of the Saxon is red with their gore,
And the mighty of nations is mighty no more.

Like a bark on the ocean long shatter'd and tost,
On the land of your fathers at length you are lost,
The hand of the spoiler is stretch'd on your plains,
And you're doomed from your cradles to bondage and chains.

Oh where is the beauty that beam'd on thy brow?
Strong hand in the battle, how weak art thou now!
That heart is now broken that never would quail,
And thy high songs are turn'd into weeping and wail.

Bright shades of our sires! from your home in the skies
Oh blast not your sons with the scorn of your eyes!
Proud spirit of Gollamh, how red is thy cheek!
For thy freemen are slaves, and thy mighty are weak!

O'Neill of the Hostages, Con, whose high name
On a hundred red battles has floated to fame,
Let the long grass still sigh undisturbed o'er thy sleep,
Arise not to shame us, awake not to weep!

In thy broad wing of darkness infold us, oh night!
Withhold, oh bright sun, the reproach of thy light!
For freedom or valour no more canst thou see,
In the home of the Brave, in the isle of the Free.

Affliction's dark waters your spirits have bow'd,
And oppression hath wrapped all your land in its shroud,
Since first from the Brehons' pure justice you stray'd,
And bent to those laws the proud Saxon has made.

We know not our country, so strange is her face,
Her sons once her glory are now her disgrace;
Gone, gone is the beauty of fair Innisfail,
For the stranger now rules in the land of the Gael.

Where, where are the woods that oft rung to your cheer,
Where you waked the wild chase of the wolf and the deer?
Can those dark heights, with ramparts all frowning and riven,
Be the hills where your forests waved brightly in Heaven?

Oh bondsmen of Egypt, no Moses appears
To light your dark steps thro' this desert of tears;
Degraded and lost ones, no Hector is nigh,
To lead you to freedom, or teach you to die!

—*translated by Jeremiah Joseph Callanan*

ANONYMOUS

Dirge of O'Sullivan Bear

One of the Sullivans of Bearhaven, who went by the name of Morty Oge, fell under the vengeance of the law. He had long been a very popular character in the wild district which he inhabited, and was particularly obnoxious to the local authorities, who had good reason to suspect him of enlisting men for the Irish Brigade in the French service, in which it was said he held a captain's commission. Information of his raising these "Wild Geese" (the name by which such recruits were known) was given by a Mr. Puxley, on whom, in consequence, O'Sullivan vowed revenge, which he executed by shooting him on Sunday while on his way to church. This called for the interposition of the higher powers, and accordingly a party of military was sent round from Cork to attack O'Sullivan's house. He was daring and well armed; and the house was fortified, so that he made an obstinate defence. At last a confidential servant of his, named Scully, was bribed to wet the powder in the guns and pistols prepared for his defence, which rendered him powerless. He attempted to escape, but while springing over a high wall in the rear of his house he received a mortal wound in the back. They tied his body to a boat, and dragged it in that manner through the sea from Bearhaven to Cork, where his head was cut off, and fixed on the county jail, where it remained for several years. (Note by J. J. Callanan; the poem was composed in the late seventeenth century)

The sun on Ivera*
    No longer shines brightly;
The voice of her music
    No longer is sprightly;
No more to her maidens
    The light dance is dear,
Since the death of our darling
    O'Sullivan Bear.

*The old name of Bearhaven; it is still preserved in the name of the barony of Iveragh.—
Callanan.

Scully! thou false one,
　　You basely betrayed him,
In his strong hour of need,
　　When thy right hand should aid him;
He fed thee—he clad thee—
　　You had all could delight thee:
You left him—you sold him—
　　May heaven requite thee!

Scully! may all kinds
　　Of evil attend thee!
On thy dark road of life
　　May no kind one befriend thee!
May fevers long burn thee,
　　And agues long freeze thee!
May the strong hand of God
　　In his red anger seize thee!

Had he died calmly,
　　I would not deplore him;
Or if the wild strife
　　Of the sea-war closed o'er him:
But with ropes round his white limbs
　　Through ocean to trail him,
Like a fish after slaughter—
　　'Tis therefore I wail him.

Long may the curse
　　Of his people pursue them;
Scully, that sold him,
　　And soldier that slew him!
One glimpse of heaven's light
　　May they see never!
May the hearthstone of hell
　　Be their best bed for ever!

In the hole which the vile hands
　　Of soldiers had made thee,
Unhonour'd, unshrouded,
　　And headless they laid thee;
No sigh to regret thee,
　　No eye to rain o'er thee,
No dirge to lament thee,
　　No friend to deplore thee!

Dear head of my darling,
　　How gory and pale,

These aged eyes see thee,
   High spiked on their gaol!
That cheek in the summer sun
   Ne'er shall grow warm;
Nor that eye e'er catch light,
   But the flash of the storm.

A curse, blessed ocean,
   Is on thy green water,
From the haven of Cork,
   To Ivera of slaughter:
Since thy billows were dyed
   With the red wounds of fear
Of Muiertach Oge,*
   Our O'Sullivan Bear!

     —translated by Jeremiah Joseph Callanan

MAURICE DUGAN (dates unknown)

Some time around 1640, Dugan was alive and composed this song, whose title in Irish, "An chúil-fhionn," means the maiden of fair flowing locks.

The Coolun

O, had you seen the Coolun,
   Walking down by the cuckoo's street,
With the dew of the meadows shining
   On her milk-white twinkling feet.
O, my love she is, and my *cailin óg*,†
   And she dwells in Bal'nagar;
And she bears the palm of beauty bright,
   From the fairest that in Erin are.

In Bal'nagar is the Coolun,
   Like the berry on the bough her cheek;
Bright beauty dwells for ever
   On her fair neck and ringlets sleek;
O, sweeter is her mouth's soft music
   Than the lark or thrush at dawn,
Or the blackbird in the greenwood singing
   Farewell to the setting sun.

*Young Morty.
†[cailin óg, young girl.

Rise up, my boy! make ready
  My horse, for I forth would ride,
To follow the modest damsel,
  Where she walks on the green hill-side:
For e'er since our youth were we plighted,
  In faith, troth, and wedlock true—
O, she's sweeter to me than nine times over,
  Than organ or cuckoo!

O, ever since my childhood
  I loved the fair and darling child;
But our people came between us,
  And with lucre our pure love defiled:
O, my woe it is, and my bitter pain,
  And I weep it night and day,
That the *cailin bán* of my early love
  Is torn from my heart away.

Sweetheart and faithful treasure,
  Be constant still, and true;
Nor for want of herds and houses
  Leave one who would ne'er leave you.
I'll pledge you the blessed Bible,
  Without and eke within,
That the faithful God will provide for us,
  Without thanks to kith or kin.

O, love, do you remember
  When we lay all night alone,
Beneath the ash in the winter storm,
  When the oak wood round did groan?
No shelter then from the blast had we,
  The bitter blast or sleet,
But your gown to wrap about our heads,
  And my coat around our feet.

—*translated by Samuel Ferguson*

ANONYMOUS

Dear Dark Head

This verse is from a folk song composed in the eighteenth century.

Put your head, darling, darling, darling,
    Your darling black head my heart above;
Oh, mouth of honey, with the thyme for fragrance,
    Who with heart in breast could deny you love?

Oh, many and many a young girl for me is pining,
    Letting her locks of gold to the cold wind free,
For me, the foremost of our gay young fellows;
    But I'd leave a hundred, pure love, for thee!

Then put your head, darling, darling, darling,
    Your darling black head my heart above;
Oh, mouth of honey, with the thyme for fragrance,
    Who, with heart in breast, could deny you love?

—*translated by Samuel Ferguson*

Cashel of Munster

This verse is from a folk song, circa eighteenth century.

I'd wed you without herds, without money, or rich array,
And I'd wed you on a dewy morning at day-dawn grey;
My bitter woe it is, love, that we are not far away
In Cashel town, though the bare deal board were our marriage-bed this
    day.

Oh, fair maid, remember the green hill side,
Remember how I hunted about the valleys wide;
Time now has worn me; my locks are turned to grey,
The year is scarce and I am poor, but send me not, love, away!

Oh, deem not my birth is of base strain, my girl,
Oh, deem not my birth was as the birth of a churl;
Marry me, and prove me, and say soon you will,
That noble blood is written on my right side still!

My purse holds no red gold, no coin of the silver white,
No herds are mine to drive through the long twilight!
But the pretty girl that would take me, all bare though I be and lone,
Oh, I'd take her with me kindly to the county Tyrone.

Oh, my girl, I can see 'tis in trouble you are,
And, oh, my girl, I see 'tis your people's reproach you bear;
"I am a girl in trouble for his sake with whom I fly,
And, oh, may no other maiden know such reproach as I!"

—translated by Samuel Ferguson

Pearl of the White Breast

This verse is from an anonymous folk song, circa eighteenth century.

There's a colleen fair as May,
For a year and for a day,
  I've sought by every way her heart to gain
There's no art of tongue or eye
Fond youths with maidens try,
  But I've tried with ceaseless sigh, yet tried in vain.

If to France or far-off Spain
She'd cross the watery main,
  To see her face again the sea I'd brave.
And if 'tis Heaven's decree
That mine she may not be,
  May the Son of Mary me in mercy save!

O thou blooming milk-white dove,
To whom I've given true love,
  Do not ever thus reprove my constancy.
There are maidens would be mine,
With wealth in hand and kine,
  If my heart would but incline to turn from thee.

But a kiss with welcome bland
And a touch of thy dear hand
  Are all that I demand, wouldst thou not spurn;
For if not mine, dear girl,
O Snowy-Breasted Pearl!
  May I never from the fair with life return!

—translated by George Petrie

The Convict of Clonmel

This verse is from a folk song, circa eighteenth century.

How hard is my fortune,
   And vain my repining!
The strong rope of fate
   For this young neck is twining.
My strength is departed;
   My cheek sunk and sallow;
While I languish in chains,
   In the goal of Clonmala.

No boy in the village
   Was ever yet milder,
I'd play with a child,
   And my sport would be wilder.
I'd dance without tiring
   From morning till even,
And the goal-ball I'd strike
   To the lightning of Heaven.

At my bed-foot decaying,
   My hurlbat is lying,
Through the boys of the village
   My goal-ball is flying;
My horse 'mong the neighbours
   Neglected may fallow,—
While I pine in my chains,
   In the gaol of Clonmala.

Next Sunday the patron
   At home will be keeping,
And the young active hurlers
   The field will be sweeping.
With the dance of fair maidens
   The evening they'll hallow,
While this heart, once so gay,
   Shall be cold in Clonmala.

—translated by Jeremiah Joseph Callanan

EILEEN O'CONNELL (dates unknown)

Eileen O'Connell, known as "Dark Eileen," or "Eileen of the Raven Locks," was the wife of Arthur O'Leary. O'Leary had been an officer in the Hungarian service, but returned to his land in County Cork. A neighbor, whose horse had been beaten in a race by O'Leary's mare, took advantage of the Penal Laws, which did not permit a Catholic to possess a horse valued at more than five pounds. The neighbor demanded the mare from O'Leary for this sum. O'Leary refused, saying that he "would surrender his mare only with his life." In May 1773 a local magistrate proclaimed O'Leary an outlaw; English soldiers were sent to lie in wait for him as he was returning home at night, and he was shot through the heart. He was twenty-six years old. Eileen was informed of her husband's death by the return of the mare without its rider. (Note by Eleanor Hull)

Dirge on the Death of Art O'Leary
Shot at Carraganime, Co. Cork, May 4, 1773

I

My closest and dearest!
From the first day I saw you
From the top of the market-house,
My eyes gave heed to you,
My heart gave affection to you,
I fled from my friends with you,
Far from my home with you,
No lasting sorrow this to me.

II

Thou didst bring me to fair chambers,
Rooms you had adorned for me;
Ovens were reddened for me,
Fresh trout were caught for me,
Roast flesh was carved for me
From beef that was felled for me;
On beds of down I lay
Till the coming of the milking-time,
Or so long as was pleasing to me.

III

Rider of the white palm!
With the silver-hilted sword!
Well your beaver hat became you
With its band of graceful gold;

Your suit of solid homespun yarn
Wrapped close around your form;
Slender shoes of foreign fashion,
And a pin of brightest silver
Fastened in your shirt.
As you rode in stately wise
On your slender steed, white-faced,
After coming over seas,
Even the Saxons bowed before you
Bowed down to the very ground;
Not because they loved you well
But from deadly hate;
For it was by them you fell,
Darling of my soul.

IV

My friend and my little calf!
Offspring of the Lords of Antrim,
And the chiefs of Immokely!
Never had I thought you dead,
Until there came to me your mare
Her bridle dragged beside her to the ground;
Upon her brow your heart-blood splashed,
Even to the carven saddle flowing down
Where you were wont to sit or stand.
I did not stay to cleanse it—
I gave a quick leap with my hands
Upon the wooden stretcher of the bed;
A second leap was to the gate,
And the third leap upon thy mare.

V

In haste I clapped my hands together,
I followed on your tracks
As well as I could,
Till I found you laid before me dead
At the foot of a lowly bush of furze;
Without pope, without bishop,
Without cleric or priest
To read a psalm for thee;
But only an old bent wasted crone
Who flung over thee the corner of her cloak.

VI

My dear and beloved one!
When it will come to me to reach our home,
Little Conor, of our love,
And Fiac, his toddling baby-brother,
Will be asking of me quickly
Where I left their dearest father?
I shall answer them with sorrow
That I left him in Kill Martyr;
They will call upon their father;
He will not be there to answer.

VII

My love and my chosen one!
When you were going forward from the gate,
You turned quickly back again!
You kissed your two children,
You threw a kiss to me.
You said, "Eileen, arise now, be stirring,
And set your house in order,
Be swiftly moving.
I am leaving our home,
It is likely that I may not come again."
I took it only for a jest
You used often to be jesting thus before.

VIII

My friend and my heart's love!
Arise up, my Art,
Leap on thy steed,
Arise out to Macroom
And to Inchegeela after that;
A bottle of wine in thy grasp,
As was ever in the time of thy ancestors.
Arise up, my Art,
Rider of the shining sword;
Put on your garments,
Your fair noble clothes;
Don your black beaver,
Draw on your gloves;
See, here hangs your whip,
Your good mare waits without;
Strike eastward on the narrow road,

For the bushes will bare themselves before you,
For the streams will narrow on your path,
For men and women will bow themselves before you
If their own good manners are upon them yet,
But I am much a-feared they are not now.

IX

Destruction to you and woe,
O Morris, hideous the treachery
That took from me the man of the house,
The father of my babes;
Two of them running about the house,
The third beneath my breast,
It is likely that I shall not give it birth.

X

My long wound, my bitter sorrow,
That I was not beside thee
When the shot was fired;
That I might have got it in my soft body
Or in the skirt of my gown;
Till I would give you freedom to escape,
O Rider of the grey eye,
Because it is you would best have followed after them.

XI

My dear and my heart's love!
Terrible to me the way I see thee,
To be putting our hero,
Our rider so true of heart,
In a little cap in a coffin!
Thou who used to be fishing along the streams,
Thou who didst drink within wide halls
Among the gentle women white of breast;
It is my thousand afflictions
That I have lost your companionship!
My love and my darling,
Could my shouts but reach thee
West in mighty Derrynane,
And in Carhen of the yellow apples after that;
Many a light-hearted young horseman,
And woman with white spotless kerchief
Would swiftly be with us here,

To wail above thy head
Art O'Leary of the joyous laugh!
O women of the soft wet eyes,
Stay now your weeping,
Till Art O'Leary drinks his drink
Before his going back to school;
Not to learn reading or music does he go there now,
But to carry clay and stones.

XII

My love and my secret thou.
Thy corn-stacks are piled,
And thy golden kine are milking,
But it is upon my own heart is the grief!
There is no healing in the Province of Munster,
Nor in the Island smithy of the Fians,
Till Art O'Leary will come back to me;
But all as if it were a lock upon a trunk
And the key of it gone straying;
Or till rust will come upon the screw.

XIII

My friend and my best one!
Art O'Leary, son of Conor,
Son of Cadach, son of Lewis,
Eastward from wet wooded glens,
Westward from the slender hill
Where the rowan-berries grow,
And the yellow nuts are ripe upon the branches;
Apples trailing, as it was in my day.
Little wonder to myself
If fires were lighted in O'Leary's country,
And at the mouth of Ballingeary,
Or at holy Gougane Barra of the cells,
After the rider of the smooth grip,
After the huntsman unwearied
When, heavy breathing with the chase,
Even thy lithe deerhounds lagged behind.
O horseman of the enticing eyes,
What happened thee last night?
For I myself thought
That the whole world could not kill you
When I bought for you that shirt of mail.

XIV

My friend and my darling!
A cloudy vision through the darkness
Came to me last night,
At Cork lately
And I alone upon my bed!
I saw the wooded glen withered,
I saw our lime-washed court fallen;
No sound of speech came from thy hunting-dogs
Nor sound of singing from the birds
When you were found fallen
On the side of the hill without;
When you were found in the clay,
Art O'Leary;
With your drop of blood oozing out
Through the breast of your shirt.

XV

It is known to Jesus Christ,
I will put no cap upon my head,
Nor body-linen on my side,
Nor shoes upon my feet,
Nor gear throughout the house;
Even on the brown mare will be no bridle,
But I shall spend all in taking the law.
I will go across the seas
To speak with the king;
But if they will give no heed to me,
It is I that will come back again
To seek the villain of the black blood
Who cut off my treasure from me.
O Morrison, who killed my hero,
Was there not one man in Erin
Would put a bullet through you?

XVI

The affection of this heart to you,
O white women of the mill,
For the edged poetry that you have shed
Over the horseman of the brown mare.
It is I who am the lonely one
In Inse Carriganane.

—*translated by Eleanor Hull*

ANTHONY RAFTERY (1784–1835)

Born in County Mayo, and one of Ireland's last "wandering poets,"
Raftery was blind since childhood and made his living composing
music and poetry. He died in Craughwell, County Galway.

I Am Raftery

I am Raftery the Poet
   Full of hope and love,
With eyes that have no light,
   With gentleness that has no misery.

Going west upon my pilgrimage
   By the light of my heart,
Feeble and tired
   To the end of my road.

Behold me now,
   And my face to the wall,
A-playing music
   Unto empty pockets.

—translated by Douglas Hyde

Dust Hath Closed Helen's Eye

Going to Mass, by the will of God
The day came wet and the wind rose;
I met Mary Haynes at the cross of Kiltartan
And I fell in love with her then and there.

I spoke to her kind and mannerly
As by report was her own way;
And she said, "Raftery, my mind is easy,
You may come today to Baile-laoi."

When I heard her offer I did not linger,
When her talk went to my heart my heart rose.
We had only to go across the three fields,
We had daylight with us to Baile-laoi.

The table was laid with glasses and a quart measure;
She had fair hair and she sitting beside me,
And she said, "Drink, Raftery, and a hundred welcomes,
There is a strong cellar in Baile-laoi."

O star of light, and O sun in harvest,
O amber hair, O my share of the world,
Will you come with me upon Sunday
Till we agree together before all the people?

I would not grudge you a song every Sunday evening,
Punch on the table or wine if you would drink it,
But, O King of Glory, dry the roads before me,
Till I find the way to Baile-laoi.

There is a sweet air on the side of the hill
When you are looking down upon Baile-laoi;
When you are walking in the valley picking nuts and blackberries
There is music of the birds in it and music of the sidhe.

What is the worth of greatness till you have the light
Of the flower of the branch that is by your side?
There is no good to deny it or to try to hide it,
She is the sun in the heavens who wounded my heart.

There is no part of Ireland I did not travel
From the rivers to the tops of the mountains,
To the edge of Loch Greine whose mouth is hidden,
And I saw no beauty that was behind hers.

Her hair was shining and her brows were shining, too;
Her face was like herself, her mouth pleasant and sweet.
She is my pride, and I give her the branch,
She is the shining flower of Baile-laoi.

It is Mary Haynes, the calm and easy woman,
Her beauty in her mind and in her face.
If a hundred clerks were gathered together,
They could not write down a half of her ways.

—translated by Lady Augusta Gregory

ANONYMOUS

"O Donall Oge": The Grief of a Girl's Heart

Donall Oge, or "Young Donall," was the subject
of many folk songs, circa nineteenth century.

O Donall Oge, if you will go across the sea,
Bring myself with you, and do not forget it;
There will be a "faring" for thee on fine days and market-days,
And the daughter of the King of Greece as your bed-fellow at night.

If you go over seas, there is a token I have of you,
Your bright top-knot and your two grey eyes,
Twelve ringlets on your yellow curling head,
Like the cowslip or the rose-leaf in the garden.

You promised me, but you spoke a lie to me,
That you would be before me at the fold of the sheep;
I let a whistle out and three hundred shouts for you,
But I found nothing in it but a lamb a-bleating.

You promised me, a thing that was hard for you,
A ship of gold under a mast of silver,
Twelve great towns of the world's market-towns,
And a fine white court beside the sea.

You promised me, a thing that was not possible,
You would give me gloves of fishes' skin,
You would give me shoes of the feathers of birds,
And gowns of silk the richest in Erinn.

O Donall Oge, it were better for thee I to be with thee,
Than a high-born, arrogant, wasteful lady;
I would milk your cows and I would churn for you,
And if it went hard with you, I would strike a blow with you.

Och, ochone, it is not the hunger,
Nor want of food and drink, nor want of sleep,
That has left me wasting and weary;
The love of a young man it is that has sickened me.

Early in the morning I saw the young man
On the back of his horse going along the road;
He did not move over to me nor take any heed of me,
And on my coming home, it is I who wept my fill.

When I myself go to the Well of Loneliness
I sit down and I go through my trouble,
When I see the world and I see not my lad;
There was the shadow of amber upon his hair.

It was a Sunday that I gave my love to you,
The Sunday before Easter Sunday exactly;
I myself on my knees a-reading the Passion,
My two eyes giving love to you ever after.

Oye, little mother, give myself to him,
And give him what is yours of goods entirely,
Out with yourself a-begging alms
And do not be going East and West seeking me.

My little mother said to me not to speak with you
Today or tomorrow or on Sunday,
It is in the bad hour she gave me that choice,
It is "shutting the door after the theft."

And you passed me by, dark and late,
And you passed me by, and the light of the day in it;
If you would come in yourself and see me
Never a word at all would I have with you.

—translated by Eleanor Hull

I Shall Not Die For Thee
(nineteenth century)

For thee I shall not die,
    Woman high of fame and name;
Foolish men thou mayest slay
    I and they are not the same.

Why should I expire
    For the fire of any eye,
Slender waist or swan-like limb,
    Is't for them that I should die?

The round breasts, the fresh skin,
    Cheeks crimson, hair so long and rich;
Indeed, indeed, I shall not die,
    Please God, not I, for any such.

The golden hair, the forehead thin,
    The chaste mien, the gracious ease,
The rounded heel, the languid tone,
    Fools alone find death from these.

Thy sharp wit, thy perfect calm,
    Thy thin palm like foam of sea;
Thy white neck, thy blue eye,
    I shall not die for thee.

Woman, graceful as the swan,
    A wise man did nurture me,
Little palm, white neck, bright eye,
    I shall not die for ye.

—translated by Douglas Hyde

The Stars Stand Up

This is an anonymous nineteenth-century song.

The stars stand up in the air,
The sun and the moon are set,
The sea that ebbed dry of its tide
Leaves no single pebble wet;
The cuckoo keeps saying each hour
That she, my Storeen, is fled,—
O Girl of the brave, free tresses,
Far better had you struck me dead!

Three things have I learned through love,
Sorrow, and death, and pain,
My mind reminding me daily
I never shall see you again;
You left me no cure for my sickness,
Yet I pray, though my night be long,—
My sharp grief! and my heart is broken,—
That God may forgive your wrong.

She was sweeter than fiddle and lute,
Or the shining of grass through the dew,
She was soft as the blackbird's flute
When the light of the day is new;
From her feet on the lone hill-top
I have heard the honey dropping;
Why, Girl, did you come to my door?
Or why could you not be stopping?

—translated by Eleanor Hull

A Curse on a Closed Gate

This is an anonymous folk song, circa nineteenth century.

Be this the fate
Of the man who would shut his gate
On the stranger, gentle or simple, early or late.

When his mouth with a day's long hunger and thirst would wish
For the savour of salted fish,
Let him sit and eat his fill of an empty dish.

To the man of that ilk,
Let water stand in his churn, instead of milk
That turns a calf's coat silk.

And under the gloomy night
May never a thatch made tight
Shut out the clouds from his sight.

Above the ground or below it,
Good cheer, may he never know it,
Nor a tale by the fire, nor a dance on the road, nor a song by a
      wandering poet.

Till he open his gate
To the stranger, early or late,
And turn back the stone of his fate.

                            —*translated by James H. Cousins*

Pastheen Finn

*The title of this folk song means "Fair Little Child." It
was recorded and translated in the nineteenth century.*

Oh, my fair Pastheen is my heart's delight,
Her gay heart laughs in her blue eye bright;
Like the apple blossom her bosom white,
And her neck like the swan's on a March morn bright!
    Then, Oro, come with me! come with me!
      come with me!
      Oro, come with me! brown girl, sweet!
      And oh! I would go through snow and sleet,
      If you would come with me, brown girl, sweet!

Love of my heart, my fair Pastheen!
Her cheeks are as red as the rose's sheen,
But my lips have tasted no more, I ween,
Than the glass I drank to the health of my queen!
    Then, Oro, come with me! come with me!
      come with me!
      Oro, come with me! brown girl, sweet!
      And oh! I would go through snow and sleet,
      If you would come with me, brown girl, sweet!

Were I in the town, where's mirth and glee,
Or 'twixt two barrels of barley bree,
With my fair Pastheen upon my knee,
'Tis I would drink to her pleasantly!
    Then, Oro, come with me! come with me!
      come with me!

Oro, come with me! brown girl, sweet!
And oh! I would go through snow and sleet,
If you would come with me, brown girl, sweet!

Nine nights I lay in longing and pain,
Betwixt two bushes, beneath the rain,
Thinking to see you, love, once again;
But whistle and call were all in vain!
    Then, Oro, come with me! come with me!
        come with me!
    Oro, come with me! brown girl, sweet!
    And oh! I would go through snow and sleet,
    If you would come with me, brown girl, sweet!

I'll leave my people, both friend and foe;
From all the girls in the world I'll go;
But from you, sweetheart, oh, never! oh, no!
Till I lie in the coffin, stretched cold and low!
    Then, Oro, come with me! come with me!
        come with me!
    Oro, come with me! brown girl, sweet!
    And oh! I would go through snow and sleet,
    If you would come with me, brown girl, sweet!

—translated by Samuel Ferguson

II. Anonymous Street Songs and Ballads

The Night Before Larry Was Stretched

This poem was written in the Dublin slang of the eighteenth century by some anonymous Villon. At the time there were many songs celebrating life in the gaol and the business of an execution. The coffin was usually sent into the condemned cell "that the sight might suggest the immediate prospect of death and excite corresponding feelings of solemn reflection and preparation for the awful event." The friends of the condemned man were allowed to be with him before the execution, and the coffin was generally used as a card table. (Note by Padraic Colum)

The night before Larry was stretched,
The boys they all paid him a visit;
A bait in their sacks, too, they fetched;
They sweated their duds till they riz it:
For Larry was ever the lad,
When a boy was condemned to the squeezer,
Would fence all the duds that he had
To help a poor friend to a sneezer,
And warm his gob 'fore he died.

The boys they came crowding in fast,
They drew all their stools round about him,
Six glims round his trap-case were placed,
He couldn't be well waked without 'em.
When one of us asked could he die
Without having truly repented,
Says Larry, "That's all in my eye;
And first by the clargy invented,
To get a fat bit for themselves."

"I'm sorry, dear Larry," says I,
"To see you in this situation;
And blister my limbs if I lie,
I'd as lieve it had been my own station."
"Ochone! it's all all over," says he,
"For the neck-cloth I'll be forced to put on,
And by this time tomorrow you'll see

49

Your poor Larry as dead as a mutton,
Because, why, his courage was good.

"And I'll be cut up like a pie,
And my nob from my body be parted."
"You're in the wrong box, then," says I,
"For blast me if they're so hard-hearted;
A chalk on the back of your neck
Is all that Jack Ketch dares to give you;
Then mind not such trifles a feck,
For why should the likes of them grieve you?
And now, boys, come tip us the deck."

The cards being called for, they played,
Till Larry found one of them cheated;
A dart at his napper he made
(The boy being easily heated);
"Oh, by the hokey, you thief,
I'll scuttle your nob with my daddle!
You cheat me because I'm in grief,
But soon I'll demolish your noddle,
And leave you your claret to drink."

Then the clergy came in with his book,
He spoke him so smooth and so civil;
Larry tipped him a Kilmainham look,
And pitched his big wig to the devil;
Then sighing, he threw back his head,
To get a sweet drop of the bottle,
And pitiful sighing, he said:
"Oh, the hemp will be soon round my throttle,
And choke my poor windpipe to death.

"Though sure it's the best way to die,
Oh, the devil a better a-living!
For, sure when the gallows is high
Your journey is shorter to heaven:
But what harasses Larry the most,
And makes his poor soul melancholy,
Is to think on the time when his ghost
Will come in a sheet to sweet Molly—
Oh, sure it will kill her alive!"

So moving these last words he spoke,
We all vented our tears in a shower;
For my part, I thought my heart broke,
To see him cut down like a flower.

On his travels we watched him next day,
Oh, the throttler! I thought I could kill him;
But Larry not one word did say,
Nor changed till he came to "King William"—
Then, musha! his color grew white.

When he came to the nubbling chit,
He was tucked up so neat and so pretty,
The rumbler jogged off from his feet,
And he died with his feet to the city;
He kicked, too—but that was all pride,
But soon you might see 'twas all over;
Soon after the noose was untied,
And at darky we waked him in clover,
And sent him to take a ground sweat.

Nell Flaherty's Drake
*This verse is from a "street song," or folk ballad,
of the eighteenth or nineteenth century.*

My name it is Nell, right candid I tell,
   And I live near a dell I ne'er will deny,
I had a large drake, the truth for to spake,
   My grandfather left me when going to die;
He was merry and sound, and would weigh twenty pound,
   The universe round would I rove for his sake.
Bad luck to the robber, be he drunken or sober,
   That murdered Nell Flaherty's beautiful drake.

His neck it was green, and rare to be seen,
   He was fit for a queen of the highest degree.
His body so white, it would you delight,
   He was fat, plump, and heavy, and brisk as a bee.
This dear little fellow, his legs they were yellow,
   He could fly like a swallow, or swim like a hake,
But some wicked habbage, to grease his white cabbage,
   Has murdered Nell Flaherty's beautiful drake!

May his pig never grunt, may his cat never hunt,
   That a ghost may him haunt in the dark of the night.
May his hens never lay, may his horse never neigh,
   May his goat fly away like an old paper kite;
May his duck never quack, may his goose be turned black
   And pull down his stack with her long yellow beak.
May the scurvy and itch never part from the britch
   Of the wretch that murdered Nell Flaherty's drake!

May his rooster ne'er crow, may his bellows not blow,
 Nor potatoes to grow—may he never have none—
May his cradle not rock, may his chest have no lock,
 May his wife have no frock for to shade her backbone.
That the bugs and the fleas may this wicked wretch tease,
 And a piercing north breeze make him tremble and shake.
May a four-years'-old bug build a nest in the lug
 Of the monster that murdered Nell Flaherty's drake.

May his pipe never smoke, may his tea-pot be broke,
 And to add to the joke may his kettle not boil;
May he be poorly fed till the hour he is dead.
 May he always be fed on lobscouse and fish oil.
May he swell with the gout till his grinders fall out,
 May he roar, howl, and shout with a horrid toothache,
May his temple wear horns and his toes carry corns,
 The wretch that murdered Nell Flaherty's drake.

May his dog yelp and howl with both hunger and cold,
 May his wife always scold till his brains go astray.
May the curse of each hag, that ever carried a bag,
 Light down on the wag till his head it turns gray.
May monkeys still bite him, and mad dogs affright him,
 And every one slight him, asleep or awake.
May wasps ever gnaw him, and jackdaws ever claw him,
 The monster that murdered Nell Flaherty's drake.

But the only good news I have to diffuse,
 Is of Peter Hughes and Paddy McCade,
And crooked Ned Manson, and big-nosed Bob Hanson,
 Each one had a grandson of my beautiful drake.
Oh! my bird he has dozens of nephews and cousins,
 And one I must have, or my heart it will break.
To keep my mind easy, or else I'll run crazy,
 And so ends the song of my beautiful drake.

Johnny, I Hardly Knew Ye
This is a street ballad, circa 1800.

 While going the road to sweet Athy,
   Hurroo! hurroo!
 While going the road to sweet Athy,
   Hurroo! hurroo!
 While going the road to sweet Athy,
 A stick in my hand and a drop in my eye,

A doleful damsel I heard cry:—
"Och, Johnny, I hardly knew you.
With drums and guns and guns and drums,
    The enemy nearly slew ye,
    My darling dear, you look so queer,
Och, Johnny, I hardly knew ye!

"Where are your eyes that looked so mild?
    Hurroo! hurroo!
Where are your eyes that looked so mild?
    Hurroo! hurroo!
Where are your eyes that looked so mild,
When my poor heart you first beguiled?
Why did you run from me and the child?
    Och, Johnny, I hardly knew ye!
With drums, etc.

"Where are the legs with which you run?
    Hurroo! hurroo!
Where are the legs with which you run?
    Hurroo! hurroo!
Where are the legs with which you run,
When you went to carry a gun?—
Indeed, your dancing days are done!
    Och, Johnny, I hardly knew ye!
With drums, etc.

"It grieved my heart to see you sail,
    Hurroo! hurroo!
It grieved my heart to see you sail,
    Hurroo! hurroo!
It grieved my heart to see you sail,
Though from my heart you took leg bail,—
Like a cod you're doubled up head and tail.
    Och, Johnny, I hardly knew ye!
With drums, etc.

"You haven't an arm and you haven't a leg,
    Hurroo! hurroo!
You haven't an arm and you haven't a leg,
    Hurroo! hurroo!
You haven't an arm and you haven't a leg,
You're an eyeless, noseless, chickenless egg;
You'll have to be put in a bowl to beg:
    Och, Johnny, I hardly knew ye!
With drums, etc.

"I'm happy for to see you home,
    Hurroo! hurroo!
I'm happy for to see you home,
    Hurroo! hurroo!
I'm happy for to see you home,
All from the island of Sulloon,*
So low in flesh, so high in bone,
    Och, Johnny, I hardly knew ye!
With drums, etc.

"But sad as it is to see you so,
    Hurroo! hurroo!
But sad as it is to see you so,
    Hurroo! hurroo!
But sad as it is to see you so,
And to think of you now as an object of woe,
Your Peggy'll still keep ye on as her beau;
    Och, Johnny, I hardly knew ye!

"With drums and guns and guns and drums,
    The enemy nearly slew ye,
    My darling dear, you look so queer,
Och, Johnny, I hardly knew ye!"

The Irish Sailor
This is a street ballad from 1820.

All you young men, I pray attend to these few lines I write,
My mind being bent on rambling, to England I took my flight;
I being young and foolish, at home I could not stay,
But left my tender parents, and from them stole away.

I hired with a merchant of honour and renown;
I lived with him quite happy till fortune seemed to frown;
He had a handsome daughter, few to her could compare,
This lady fell in love with me, and now is in despair.

But when her father came to her the truth she has made known;
He found she loved me dearly, which made him for to frown.
Said he, "I'll soon prevent her, and that without delay;
I'll send him out in my own ship that's shortly bound for sea."

The lady was distracted, to her bedchamber flew:—
She says, "My lovely Jemmy, then must I die for you!

*Ceylon.

Some noble knights of honour their offers I did deny;—
My life I now would give to embrace my sailor boy!"

    •   •   •   •   •

But, O, my cruel parents, for sake of earthly store,
They sent my darling boy from me where the seas do loudly roar;
He was both neat and slender, he was my chiefest joy;
No lord or nobleman I see like my Irish sailor boy.

One evening as I chanced to roam along the pleasant strand,
I saw my father's ship arrive, the captain he did land;
I went to him without delay, and offered fifty pound
All for to let my father know young Jemmy he was drowned.

He kindly did embrace it, and now he's gone away;
Great tidings to him he has brought that's happened on the sea;
But when the same he did relate, great joy it did afford,
That Jemmy by a swelling wave had been swept overboard.

I walked along quite easy till I came to the quay,
Where I embraced my sailor boy and blest the happy day;
But to make my father sure believe that he lay in the deep,
When returning home again I bitterly did weep.

That night when all was silent I made good use of time;
Full fifteen thousand pounds I stole while they were drinking wine;
In his absence I proved loyal, and crowned our nuptial joy,
I bid farewell to sorrow, and wed my sailor boy.

John McGoldrick's Trial for the Quaker's Daughter
This is a street ballad from 1826.

You muses nine, with me combine; assist me with your aid,
Whilst here I am endeavouring to praise a lovely maid.
Her heart and mine were bound in love, as you may understand;
It was her whole intention to join in wedlock band.
I hope you'll pay attention, and the truth to you I'll tell;
She was a quaker's daughter, a maid I loved right well;
We being not of one persuasion, her father made a plan,
He done his whole endeavour to hang me in the wrong.
My name is John McGoldrick, the same I'll ne'er deny,—
They swore I was a radical; condemned I was to die.
As soon as my dead letter came, my sorrows did renew,
Saying, "For to die I do deny. Brave boys, what shall I do?"
At length my dearest jewel became servant in the jail;
She found her opportunity and did it not conceal.
She says, "Young John McGoldrick, I hope to be your wife;

I will do my best endeavour to save your precious life."
That night the god of Bacchus to the jailer did appear,
All with a club of gentlemen inviting him to beer.
They had the strongest liquor and the very best of wine,
The jailer and the turnkey to sleep they did incline.—
"Now, young John McGoldrick, I hope you will agree,
And bind yourself with an oath, and come along with me;
For I have stole the jailer's keys, and I could do no more."—
That very night I took my flight out of the prison door.—
Early the next morning the hurry it begun,
The 66th pursued us without either fife or drum.
The jailer and the turnkey they quickly ran us down,
And brought us back as prisoners once more to Cavan town.
There we lay bewailing, all in a prison bound,
With heavy bolts of iron secured unto the ground.
All for a second trial they brought us to the jail;
Their intention was to hang me, and send her to New South Wales.
But I may thank Lord Corry, and his father, Lord Belmore—
Long may they live in splendour around Lough Erne shore!—
They sent me a grand character, as plainly you may see,
Which caused the judge and jury that day to set us free.
You reader, now excuse me, I did refine my quill,
The praises of a lovely maid these papers for to fill.
For I have become her husband, and she my loving wife,
In spite of her old father, she saved my precious life.

III. *Poetry in English Since Swift*

JONATHAN SWIFT (1667–1745)
Swift was the famous author of Gulliver's Travels, *and cantankerous dean of Dublin's St. Patrick's Cathedral.*

An Excellent New Song on a Seditious Pamphlet*
Swift wrote this satire in 1720.

Brocades and damasks and tabbies and gauzes
    Are by Robert Ballantine lately brought over,
With forty things more: now hear what the law says,
    "Whoe'er will not wear them is not the king's lover."
        Though a printer and Dean
        Seditiously mean
Our true Irish hearts from Old England to wean,
    We'll buy English silks for our wives and our daughters,
    In spite of his Deanship and journeyman Waters.

In England the dead in woollen are clad,†
    The Dean and his printer then let us cry "fie on;"
To be clothed like a carcass would make a teague mad,
    Since a living dog better is than a dead lion.
        Our wives they grow sullen
        At wearing of woollen,
And all we poor shopkeepers must our horns pull in.
    Then we'll buy English silks for our wives and our daughters,
    In spite of his Deanship and journeyman Waters.

---

*After having written a pamphlet, advising the people of Ireland to wear their own manufactures only, and not to use those of England, a prosecution for sedition was instituted against Waters (the printer of the work), which was carried on with so much virulence, that Lord Chief Justice Whitshed kept the jury in over twelve hours, and sent them eleven times out of court, till he wearied them into a verdict of guilty. *(Note by H. Halliday Sparling)*
†A statute for the encouragement of the woollen manufacture made this compulsory.

Whoever our trading with England would hinder,
    To inflame both the nations does plainly conspire;
Because Irish linen will soon turn to tinder,
    And wool, it is greasy, and quickly takes fire.
        Therefore, I assure ye,
        Our noble grand jury,
When they saw the Dean's book they were in a great fury;
    They would buy English silks for their wives and their daughters,
    In spite of his Deanship and journeyman Waters.

That wicked rogue Waters, who always is sinning,
    And before *Coram Nobis** so oft has been called,
Henceforward, shall print neither pamphlets nor linen,
    And, if swearing can do't, shall be swingingly mauled;
        And as for the Dean,
        You know whom I mean,
If the printer will 'peach him he'll scarce come off clean.
    Then we'll buy English silks for our wives and our daughters,
    In spite of his Deanship and journeyman Waters.

Verses Made for Women Who Cry Apples, etc.

APPLES

Come buy my fine wares,
Plumbs, apples, and pears,
A hundred a penny,
In conscience too many:
Come, will you have any?
My children are seven,
I wish them in Heaven;
My husband's a sot,
With his pipe and his pot,
Nor a farthing will gain 'em,
And I must maintain 'em.

ASPARAGUS

Ripe 'sparagrass,
Fit for lad or lass,

Coram Nobis—i.e., before the Queen's Bench.

To make their water pass:
O! tis pretty picking
With a tender chicken.

❧

ONIONS

Come, follow me by the smell,
Here's delicate onions to sell,
I promise to use you well.
They make the blood warmer;
You'll feed like a farmer;
For this is every cook's opinion,
No savoury dish without an onion:
But lest your kissing should be spoil'd,
Your onions must be th'roughly boil'd;
Or else you may spare
Your mistress a share,
   The secret will never be known;
She cannot discover
The breath of her lover,
   But think it as sweet as her own.

❧

OYSTERS

Charming oysters I cry,
My masters, come buy;
So plump and so fresh,
So sweet is their flesh,
No Colchester oyster
Is sweeter and moister.
Your stomach they settle,
And rouse up your mettle:
They'll make you a dad
Of a lass or a lad;
And madam, your wife,
They'll please to the life:
Be she barren, be she old,
Be she slut, or be she scold,
Eat my oysters and lie near her,
She'll be fruitful, never fear her.

---

*Malahide, about five miles from Dublin, famous for herrings.

෪

HERRINGS

Be not sparing
Leave off swearing:
Buy my herring
Fresh from Malahide*,
Better ne'er was tried.
Come eat 'em with pure fresh butter and mustard,
Their bellies are soft, and as white as a custard.
Come, sixpence a dozen to get me some bread,
Or, like my own herrings, I soon shall be dead.

෪

ORANGES

Come buy my fine oranges, sauce for your veal,
And charming when squeez'd in a pot of brown ale:
Well roasted with sugar and wine in a cup,
They'll make a sweet bishop, when gentlefolks sup.

To Quilca: A Country-house of Dr. Sheridan, in No Very Good Repair, Where the Author and Some of His Friends Spent a Summer in the Year 1725

Let me thy properties explain:
A rotten cabin dropping rain;
Chimnies with scorn rejecting smoke;
Stools, tables, chairs, and bedsteads, broke.
Here elements have lost their uses,
Air ripens not, nor earth produces:
In vain we make poor Sheelah toil,
Fire will not roast, nor water boil.
Through all the vallies, hills, and plains,
The goddess Want in triumph reigns,
And her chief officers of state,
Sloth, Dirt, and Theft, around her wait.

WILLIAM DRENNAN (1754–1820)

Drennan was a Belfast-born poet, essayist, and physician.
He was the first writer to call Ireland "The Emerald Isle."

Eire

When Eire first rose from the dark-swelling flood,
God blessed the green island, and saw it was good;
The emerald of Europe, it sparkled and shone,
In the ring of the world, the most precious stone.
In her sun, in her soil, in her station thrice blest,
With her back towards Britain, her face to the west,
Eire stands proudly insular, on her steep shore,
And strikes her high harp 'mid the ocean's deep roar.

But when its soft tones seem to mourn and to weep,
A dark chain of silence is thrown o'er the deep;
At the thought of the past the tears gush from her eyes,
And the pulse of her heart makes her white bosom rise.
O! sons of green Eire, lament o'er the time
When religion was war, and our country a crime;
When man in God's image inverted his plan,
And moulded his God in the image of man.

When the interest of state wrought the general woe,
The stranger a friend, and the native a foe;
While the mother rejoiced o'er her children oppressed,
And clasped the invader more close to her breast;
When, with Pale for the body and Pale for the soul,
Church and State joined in compact to conquer the whole;
And, as Shannon was stained with Milesian blood,
Eyed each other askance and pronounced it was good.

By the groans that ascend from your forefathers' grave,
For their country thus left to the brute and the slave,
Drive the demon of Bigotry home to his den,
And where Britain made brutes now let Eire make men.
Let my sons like the leaves of the shamrock unite,
A partition of sects from one footstalk of right,
Give each his full share of the earth and the sky,
Nor fatten the slave where the serpent would die.

Alas! for poor Eire, that some are still seen
Who would dye the grass red from their hatred to Green;
Yet, O! when you're up and they're down, let them live,
Then yield them that mercy which they would not give.

Arm of Eire, be strong! but be gentle as brave!
And, uplifted to strike, be still ready to save!
Let no feeling of vengeance presume to defile
The cause of, or men of, the Emerald Isle.

The cause it is good, and the men they are true,
And the Green shall outlive both the Orange and Blue!
And the triumphs of Eire her daughters shall share,
With the full swelling chest, and the fair flowing hair.
Their bosom heaves high for the worthy and brave,
But no coward shall rest on that soft-swelling wave;
Men of Eire! awake, and make haste to be blest,
Rise—Arch of the Ocean, and Queen of the West!

ANDREW CHERRY (1762–1812)
Cherry was a playwright, born in Limerick.

The Green Little Shamrock of Ireland

There's a dear little plant that grows in our isle,
    'Twas St. Patrick himself sure that set it;
And the sun on his labour with pleasure did smile,
    And with dew from his eye often wet it.
It thrives through the bog, through the brake, and the mireland;
And he called it the dear little shamrock of Ireland—
    The sweet little shamrock, the dear little shamrock,
    The sweet little, green little, shamrock of Ireland!

This dear little plant still grows in our land,
    Fresh and fair as the daughters of Erin,
Whose smiles can bewitch, whose eyes can command,
    In each climate that they may appear in;
And shine through the bog, through the brake, and the mireland;
Just like their own dear little shamrock of Ireland.
    The sweet little shamrock, the dear little shamrock,
    The sweet little, green little, shamrock of Ireland!

This dear little plant that springs from our soil,
    When its three little leaves are extended,
Denotes on one stalk we together should toil,
    And ourselves by ourselves be befriended;
And still through the bog, through the brake, and the mireland,
From one root should branch, like the shamrock of Ireland.

The sweet little shamrock, the dear little shamrock,
The sweet little, green little, shamrock of Ireland!

EDWARD LYSAGHT (1763–1810)

Lysaght was a songwriter and lawyer from County Clare.

Our Dear Native Island

May God, in whose hand is the lot of each land—
   Who rules over ocean and dry land—
Inspire our good king from his presence to fling
   Ill advisers who'd ruin our Island.
Don't we feel 'tis our dear native Island?
A fertile and fine little Island!
   May Orange and Green no longer be seen
Distain'd with the blood of our Island!

The fair ones we prize declare they despise
   Those who'd make it a slavish and vile land;
Be their smiles our reward, and we'll gallantly guard
   All the rights and delights of our Island—
For, O! 'tis a lovely green Island!
Bright beauties adorn our Island!
   At St. Patrick's command, vipers quitted our land—
But he's wanted again in our Island!

For her interest and pride, we oft fought by the side
   Of England, that haughty and high land;
Nay, we'd do so again, if she'd let us remain
   A free and a flourishing Island—
But she, like a crafty and sly land,
Dissension excites in our Island,
   And, our feuds to adjust, she'd lay in the dust
All the freedom and strength of our Island.

A few years ago (though now she says nine,
   We agreed with that surly and shy land,
That each, as a friend, should the other defend,
   And the crown be the link of each Island!
'Twas the final state-bond of each Island;
Independence we swore to each Island;
   Are we grown so absurd, as to credit her word,
When she's breaking her oath with our Island?

Let us steadily stand by our king and our land,
    And it sha'n't be a slavish or vile land;
Nor impotent Pitt unpunished commit
    An attempt on the rights of our Island.
Each voice should resound through our Island,
You're my neighbour, but, Bull, this is my land!
    Nature's favourite spot, and I'd sooner be shot,
Than surrender the rights of our Island!

CHARLES WOLFE (1791–1823)

Wolfe was a clergyman whose poem was "discovered" by Lord Byron.

The Burial of Sir John Moore

Not a drum was heard, not a funeral note,
    As his corse to the rampart we hurried;
Not a soldier discharged his farewell shot
    O'er the grave where our hero we buried.

We buried him darkly at dead of night,
    The sods with our bayonets turning,
By the struggling moonbeam's misty light,
    And the lantern dimly burning.

No useless coffin enclosed his breast,
    Not in sheet or in shroud we wound him;
But he lay like a warrior taking his rest,
    With his martial cloak around him.

Few and short were the prayers we said,
    And we spoke not a word of sorrow;
But we steadfastly gazed on the face that was dead,
    And we bitterly thought of the morrow.

We thought as we hollow'd his narrow bed,
    And smooth'd down his lonely pillow,
That the foe and the stranger would tread o'er his head,
    And we far away on the billow!

Lightly they'll talk of the spirit that's gone,
    And o'er his cold ashes upbraid him,
But little he'll reck, if they let him sleep on
    In the grave where a Briton has laid him.

But half of our heavy task was done,
    When the clock struck the hour for retiring;
And we heard the distant and random gun
    That the foe was sullenly firing.

Slowly and sadly we laid him down,
    From the field of his fame fresh and gory;
We carved not a line, and we raised not a stone—
    But we left him alone in his glory!

SAMUEL LOVER (1797–1868)
Lover was a Dublin-born novelist, musician, and songwriter.

I'm Not Myself at All!

O, I'm not myself at all, Molly dear, Molly dear,
    I'm not myself at all!
Nothin' carin', nothin' knowing, 'tis after you I'm goin',
Faith you're shadow 'tis I'm growin', Molly dear,
    And I'm not myself at all!
Th' other day I went confessin', and I asked the father's blessin',
  "But," says I, "don't give me one entirely,
For I fretted so last year but the half of me is here,
  So give the other half to Molly Brierley."
        O, I'm not myself at all!

O, I'm not myself at all, Molly dear, Molly dear,
    My appetite's so small.
I once could pick a goose, but my buttons is no use,
Faith my tightest coat is loose, Molly dear,
    And I'm not myself at all!
If thus it is I waste, you'd better, dear, make haste,
  Before your lover's gone away entirely;
If you don't soon change your mind, not a bit of me you'll find—
And what 'ud you think o' that, Molly Brierley?
        O, I'm not myself at all!

O, my shadow on the wall, Molly dear, Molly dear,
    Isn't like myself at all.
For I've got so very thin, myself says 'tisn't him,
But that purty girl so slim, Molly dear,
        And I'm not myself at all!

If thus I smaller grow, all fretting, dear, for you,
　　'Tis you should make me up the deficiency;
So just let Father Taaffe make you my better-half,
　　And you will not the worse of the addition be—
　　　　O, I'm not myself at all!

I'll be not myself at all, Molly dear, Molly dear,
　　　　Till you my own I call!
Since a change o'er me there came, sure you might change your name—
And 'twould just come to the same, Molly dear,
　　　　'Twould just come to the same:
For if you and I were one, all confusion would be gone,
　　And 'twould simplify the matter entirely;
And 'twould save us so much bother when we'd both be one another—
　　So listen now to reason, Molly Brierley.
　　　　O, I'm not myself at all!

The Whistlin' Thief

When Pat came over the hill,
　　His colleen fair to see,
His whistle low, but shrill,
　　The signal was to be;

　　　　　　　　　　(Pat whistles.)

"Mary," the mother said,
　　"Someone is whistling sure;"
Says Mary, "'Tis only the wind
　　Is whistling through the door."
　　　(Pat whistles a bit of a popular air.)

"I've lived a long time, Mary,
　　In this wide world, my dear,
But a door to whistle like *that*
　　I never yet did hear."

"But, mother, you know the fiddle
　　Hangs close beside the chink,
And the wind upon the strings
　　Is playing the tune I think."

　　　　　　　　　(The pig grunts.)

"Mary, I hear the pig,
　　Unaisy in his mind."
"But, mother, you know, they say
　　The pigs can see the wind."

"That's true enough *in the day*,
    But I think you may remark
That pigs no more nor we,
    Can see anything in the dark."

                         (The dog barks.)

"The dog is barking now,
    The fiddle can't play the tune."
"But, mother, the dogs will bark
    Whenever they see the moon."

"But how could he see the moon,
    When, you know, the dog is blind?
Blind dogs won't bark at the moon,
    Nor fiddles be played by the wind.

"I'm not such a fool as you think,
    I know very well it is Pat:—
Shut your mouth, you whistlin' thief,
    And go along home out o' that!

"And you be off to your bed,
    Don't play upon me your jeers;
For though I have lost my eyes,
    I haven't lost my ears!"

JAMES CLARENCE MANGAN (1803–1849)

Mangan was a Dublin-born poet who rose from and then sank back into poverty. The poem, based on a song, "Rosin Dubh," is an allegorical address to Ireland, at a time when the Irish were hoping for military aid from the Pope and Spain against the English.

Dark Rosaleen

O my dark Rosaleen,
    Do not sigh, do not weep!
The priests are on the ocean green,
    They march along the deep.
There's wine from the royal Pope,
    Upon the ocean green;
And Spanish ale shall give you hope,
    My dark Rosaleen!
    My own Rosaleen!

Shall glad your heart, shall give you hope,
Shall give you health and help, and hope,
   My dark Rosaleen.

Over hills, and through dales,
   Have I roamed for your sake;
All yesterday I sailed with sails
   On river and on lake.
The Erne, at its highest flood,
   I dashed across unseen,
For there was lightning in my blood,
   My dark Rosaleen!
   My own Rosaleen!
Oh! there was lightning in my blood,
Red lightning lightened through my blood,
   My dark Rosaleen!

All day long in unrest,
   To and fro do I move,
The very soul within my breast
   Is wasted for you, love!
The heart in my bosom faints
   To think of you, my Queen,
My life of life, my saint of saints,
   My dark Rosaleen!
   My own Rosaleen!
To hear, your sweet and sad complaints,
My life, my love, my saint of saints,
   My dark Rosaleen!

Woe and pain, pain and woe,
   Are my lot, night and noon,
To see your bright face clouded so,
   Like to the mournful moon.
But yet will I rear your throne
   Again in golden sheen;
'Tis you shall reign, shall reign alone,
   My dark Rosaleen!
   My own Rosaleen!
'Tis you shall have the golden throne,
'Tis you shall reign, shall reign alone,
   My dark Rosaleen!

Over dews, over sands,
    Will I fly for your weal:
Your holy, delicate white hands
    Shall girdle me with steel.
At home in your emerald bowers,
    From morning's dawn till e'en,
You'll pray for me, my flower of flowers,
    My dark Rosaleen!
    My fond Rosaleen!
You'll think of me through daylight's hours,
My virgin flower, my flower of flowers,
    My dark Rosaleen!

I could scale the blue air,
    I could plough the high hills,
Oh, I could kneel all night in prayer,
    To heal your many ills!
And one beamy smile from you
    Would float like light between
My toils and me, my own, my true,
    My dark Rosaleen!
    My fond Rosaleen!
Would give me life and soul anew,
A second life, a soul anew,
    My dark Rosaleen!

O! the Erne shall run red
    With redundance of blood,
The earth shall rock beneath our tread,
    And flames wrap hill and wood,
And gun-peal, and slogan cry
    Wake many a glen serene,
Ere you shall fade, ere you shall die,
    My dark Rosaleen!
    My own Rosaleen!
The Judgment Hour must first be nigh
Ere you can fade, ere you can die,
    My dark Rosaleen!

GERALD GRIFFIN (1803–1840)

*Born in Limerick, Griffin was the author of Ireland's
most famous nineteenth-century novel,* The Collegians.

Gille Machree

Gille machree,*
Sit down by me,
We now are joined and ne'er shall sever;
This hearth's our own,
Our hearts are one,
And peace is ours for ever!

When I was poor
Your father's door
Was closed against your constant lover;
With care and pain
I tried in vain
My fortunes to recover.
I said, "To other lands I'd roam,
Where fate may smile on me, love;"
I said, "Farewell, my own old home!"
And I said, "Farewell to thee, love!"
Sing, Gille machree, etc.

I might have said,
My mountain maid,
Come live with me, your own true lover—
I know a spot,
A silent cot,
Your friends can ne'er discover,
Where gently flows the waveless tide
By one small garden only;
Where the heron waves his wings so wide,
And the linnet sings so lonely!
Sing, Gille machree, etc.

I might have said,
My mountain maid,
A father's right was never given
True hearts to curse
With tyrant force

*Brightener of my heart.

That have been blest in heaven.
But then I said, "In after years,
   When thoughts of home shall find her,
My love may mourn with secret tears
   Her friends thus left behind her."
       Sing, Gille machree, etc.

    Oh no, I said,
    My own dear maid,
For me, though all forlorn for ever,
    That heart of thine
    Shall ne'er repine
O'er slighted duty—never.
From home and thee though wandering far,
   A dreary fate be mine, love—
I'd rather live in endless war,
   Than buy my peace with thine, love.
       Sing, Gille machree, etc.

    Far, far away,
    By night and day,
I toiled to win a golden treasure;
    And golden gains
    Repaid my pains
In fair and shining measure.
I sought again my native land,
   Thy father welcomed me, love;
I poured my gold into his hand,
   And my guerdon found in thee, love.
    Sing, Gille machree,
    Sit down by me,
We now are joined, and ne'er shall sever;
    This hearth's our own,
    Our hearts are one,
And peace is ours for ever.

ELLEN FITZSIMON (1805–1883)

*Fitzsimon was born in Dublin. She was the eldest daughter of Daniel
O'Connell, the renowned leader of the Catholic emancipation movement.*

The Woods of Kylinoe:
Song of the Irish Emigrant in North America

My heart is heavy in my breast—my eyes are full of tears,
My memory is wandering back to long departed years—
To those bright days long, long ago,
When nought I dream'd of sordid care, of worldly woe—
But roved, a gay, light-hearted boy, the woods of Kylinoe.

There, in the spring-time of my life, and spring-time of the year,
I've watched the snowdrop start from earth, the first young buds appear;
The sparkling stream o'er pebbles flow,
The modest violet, and the golden primrose blow,
Within thy deep and mossy dells, beloved Kylinoe!

'Twas there I wooed my Mary Dhuv, and won her for my bride,
Who bore me three fair daughters, and four sons, my age's pride;
Though cruel fortune was our foe,
And steep'd us to the lips in bitter want and woe,
Yet cling our hearts to those sad days we pass'd near Kylinoe.

At length, by misery bowed to earth, we left our native strand,
And crossed the wide Atlantic to this free and happy land;
Though toils we had to undergo,
Yet soon content and happy peace 'twas ours to know,
And plenty, such as never blessed our hearth near Kylinoe!

And Heaven a blessing has bestow'd more precious far than wealth,
He spared us to each other, full of years, yet strong in health;
Across the threshold when we go,
We see our children's children round us grow,
Like sapling oaks within thy woods, far distant Kylinoe.

Yet sadness clouds our hearts to think that when we are no more,
Our bones must find a resting-place far, far from Erin's shore!
For us—no funeral sad and slow—
Within the ancient abbey's burial ground shall go—
No, we must slumber far from home, far, far from Kylinoe!

Yet, oh! if spirits e'er can leave the appointed place of rest,
Once more will I revisit thee, dear Isle that I love best;
O'er thy green vales will hover slow,
And many a tearful parting blessing will bestow
On all—but most of all on thee, my native Kylinoe.

JOHN WALSH (1805–1850)

*Walsh was a schoolteacher, poet, and translator, born in Londonderry.
"Druim-fionn," white-backed, is the favourite name of a cow in Irish. The title
means "the dear brown white-backed (cow)." (Note by H. Halliday Sparling)*

Drimin Donn Dílis

O! *Drimin donn dílis!* the landlord has come,
Like a foul blast of death has he swept o'er our home;
He has withered our roof-tree—beneath the cold sky,
Poor, houseless and homeless, tonight must we lie.

My heart it is cold as the white winter's snow;
My brain is on fire, and my blood's in a glow.
O! *Drimin donn dílis!* 'tis hard to forgive
When a robber denies us the right we should live.

With my health and my strength, with hard labour and toil,
I dried the wet marsh and I tilled the harsh soil;
I moiled the long day through, from morn till even,
And I thought in my heart I'd a foretaste of heaven.

The summer shone round us above and below,
The beautiful summer that makes the flowers blow:
O! 'tis hard to forget it, and think I must bear
That strangers shall reap the reward of my care.

Your limbs they were plump then—your coat it was silk,
And never was wanted the mether of milk;
For freely it came in the calm summer's noon,
While you munched to the time of the old milking croon.

How often you left the green side of the hill,
To stretch in the shade, and to drink of the rill!
And often I freed you before the grey dawn,
From your snug little pen at the edge of the bawn.

But they racked and they ground me with tax and with rent,
Till my heart it was sore, and my life-blood was spent:
Today they have finished, and on the wide world,
With the mocking of fiends from my home was I hurled.

I knelt down three times for to utter a prayer,
But my heart it was seared, and the words were not there;
O! wild were the thoughts through my dizzy head came,
Like the rushing of wind through a forest of flame.

I bid you, old comrade, a long last farewell;
For the gaunt hand of famine has clutched us too well;
It severed the master and you, my good cow,
With a blight on his life, and a brand on his brow.

LADY HELEN SELINA DUFFERIN (1807–1867)

*Lady Dufferin was a poet, and granddaughter
of the playwright Richard Brinsley Sheridan.*

Lament of the Irish Emigrant

I'm sittin' on the stile, Mary,
    Where we sat side by side
On a bright May mornin', long ago,
    When first you were my bride:
The corn was springin' fresh and green,
    And the lark sang loud and high—
And the red was on your lip, Mary,
    And the love-light in your eye.

The place is little changed, Mary,
    The day is bright as then,
The lark's loud song is in my ear,
    And the corn is green again;
But I miss the soft clasp of your hand,
    And your breath, warm on my cheek,
And I still keep list'nin' for the words
    You never more will speak.

'Tis but a step down yonder lane,
    And the little church stands near—
The church where we were wed, Mary,
    I see the spire from here.
But the graveyard lies between, Mary,
    And my step might break your rest—
For I've laid you, darling! down to sleep,
    With your baby on your breast.

I'm very lonely now, Mary,
    For the poor make no new friends;

But, oh! they love the better still,
    The few our Father sends!
And you were all I had, Mary,
    My blessin' and my pride!
There's nothin' left to care for now,
    Since my poor Mary died.

Yours was the good, brave heart, Mary,
    That still kept hoping on,
When the trust in God had left my soul,
    And my arm's young strength was gone;
There was comfort ever on your lip,
    And the kind look on your brow—
I bless you, Mary, for that same,
    Though you cannot hear me now.

I thank you for the patient smile
    When your heart was fit to break,
When the hunger pain was gnawin' there,
    And you hid it for my sake;
I bless you for the pleasant word,
    When your heart was sad and sore—
Oh! I'm thankful you are gone, Mary,
    Where grief can't reach you more!

I'm biddin' you a long farewell,
    My Mary—kind and true!
But I'll not forget you, darling,
    In the land I'm goin' to:
They say there's bread and work for all,
    And the sun shines always there—
But I'll not forget old Ireland,
    Were it fifty times as fair!

And often in those grand old woods
    I'll sit and shut my eyes,
And my heart will travel back again
    To the place where Mary lies;
And I'll think I see the little stile
    Where we sat side by side,
And the springin' corn, and the bright May morn,
    When first you were my bride.

JOHN FRANCIS WALLER (1809–1894)

Limerick-born Waller was a lawyer and poet.

The Spinning Wheel

Mellow the moonlight to shine is beginning,
Close by the window young Eileen is spinning;
Bent over the fire her blind grandmother, sitting,
Is crooning, and moaning, and drowsily knitting:—
"Eileen, achora, I hear someone tapping."
"'Tis the ivy, dear mother, against the glass flapping."
"Eily, I surely hear somebody sighing."
"'Tis the sound, mother dear, of the summer wind dying."
Merrily, cheerily, noiselessly whirring,
Swings the wheel, spins the wheel, while the foot's stirring;
Sprightly, and brightly, and airily ringing
Thrills the sweet voice of the young maiden singing.

"What's that noise that I hear at the window, I wonder?"
"'Tis the little birds chirping the holly-bush under."
"What makes you be shoving and moving your stool on,
And singing, all wrong, that old song of 'The Coolun'?"
There's a form at the casement—the form of her true love—
And he whispers, with face bent, "I'm waiting for you, love;
Get up on the stool, through the lattice step lightly,
We'll rove in the grove, while the moon's shining brightly."
Merrily, cheerily, noiselessly whirring,
Swings the wheel, spins the wheel, while the foot's stirring;
Sprightly, and brightly, and airily ringing
Thrills the sweet voice of the young maiden singing.

The maid shakes her head, on her lips lays her fingers,
Steals up from her seat—longs to go, and yet lingers;
A frightened glance turns to her drowsy grandmother,
Puts one foot on the stool, spins the wheel with the other,
Lazily, easily, swings now the wheel round,
Slowly and lowly is heard not the reel's sound;
Noiseless and light to the lattice above her
The maid steps—then leaps to the arms of her lover.
Slower—and slower—and slower the wheel swings;
Lower—and lower—and lower the reel rings;
Ere the reel and the wheel stopped their ringing and moving,
Through the grove the young lovers by moonlight are roving.

SAMUEL FERGUSON (1810–1886)

Ferguson, the great translator of Gaelic folk songs, was born in Belfast. The subject of this poem, Thomas Osborne Davis, was one of the leaders of the Young Ireland party. He died in 1845 just as his work was beginning to have an extraordinary effect. Ferguson, who had not joined the Young Ireland party, but who was in sympathy with Davis's ideas, received the news of his death while he himself was ill; many poems were written in memory of Thomas Davis, but Ferguson's is the most exalted in feeling as well as the most Gaelic in structure. (Note by Padraic Colum)

Lament for Thomas Davis

I walked through Ballinderry in the spring-time,
    When the bud was on the tree;
And I said, in every fresh-ploughed field beholding
    The sowers striding free,
Scattering broadside forth the corn in golden plenty
    On the quick seed-clasping soil,
"Even such this day, among the fresh-stirred hearts of Erin,
Thomas Davis, is thy toil."

I sat by Ballyshannon in the summer,
    And saw the salmon leap;
And I said, as I beheld the gallant creatures
    Spring glittering from the deep,
Through the spray, and through the prone heaps striving onward
    To the calm, clear streams above,
"So seekest thou thy native founts of freedom, Thomas Davis,
    In thy brightness of strength and love."

I stood in Derrybawn in the autumn,
    And I heard the eagle call,
With a clangorous cry of wrath and lamentation
    That filled the wide mountain hall,
O'er the bare, deserted place of his plundered eyrie;
    And I said, as he screamed and soared,
"So callest thou, thou wrathful, soaring Thomas Davis,
    For a nation's rights restored!"

And, alas! to think but now, and thou art lying,
    Dear Davis, dead at thy mother's knee;
And I, no mother near, on my own sick-bed,
    That face on earth shall never see;
I may lie and try to feel that I am dreaming,
    I may lie and try to say, "Thy will be done,"
But a hundred such as I will never comfort Erin
    For the loss of the noble son!

Young husbandman of Erin's fruitful seed-time,
    In the fresh track of danger's plough!
Who will walk the heavy, toilsome, perilous furrow,
Girt with freedom's seed-sheets, now?
Who will banish with the wholesome crop of knowledge
    The daunting weed and the bitter thorn,
Now that thou thyself art but a seed for hopeful planting
    Against the Resurrection morn?

Young salmon of the flood-tide of freedom
    That swells round Erin's shore!
Thou wilt leap against their loud oppressive torrent
    Of bigotry and hate no more;
Drawn downward by their prone material instinct,
    Let them thunder on their rocks and foam—
Thou hast leapt, aspiring soul, to founts beyond their raging,
    Where troubled waters never come!

But I grieve not, Eagle of the empty eyrie,
    That thy wrathful cry is still;
And that the songs alone of peaceful mourners
    Are heard today on Earth's hill;
Better far, if brothers' war be destined for us
    (God avert that horrid day I pray),
That ere our hands be stained with slaughter fratricidal,
    Thy warm heart should be cold in clay.

But my trust is strong in God, Who made us brothers,
    That He will not suffer their right hands,
Which thou hast joined in holier rites than wedlock
    To draw opposing brands.
Oh, many a tuneful tongue that thou madest vocal
    Would lie cold and silent then;
And songless long once more, should often-widowed Erin
    Mourn the loss of her brave young men.

Oh, brave young men, my love, my pride, my promise,
    'Tis on you my hopes are set,
In manliness, in kindliness, in justice,
    To make Erin a nation yet;
Self-respecting, self-relying, self-advancing—
    In union or in severance, free and strong—
And if God grant this, then, under God, to Thomas Davis
    Let the greater praise belong.

ARTHUR GERALD GEOGHEGAN (1810–1889)

Geoghegan was a Dublin-born poet and antiquarian.

The Mountain Fern

Oh, the Fern! the Fern!—the Irish hill Fern!—
That girds our blue lakes from Lough Ine to Lough Erne,
That waves on our crags like the plume of a king,
And bends, like a nun, over clear well and spring!
The fairy's tall palm tree! the heath-bird's fresh nest,
And the couch the red deer deems the sweetest and best,
With the free winds to fan it, and dew-drops to gem,—
Oh, what can ye match with this beautiful stem?

From the shrine of Saint Finbar, by lone Avonbuie,
To the halls of Dunluce, with its towers by the sea,
From the hill of Knockthu to the rath of Moyvore,
Like a chaplet it circles our green island o'er—
In the bawn of the chief, by the anchorite's cell,
On the hill-top, or greenwood, by streamlet or well,
With a spell on each leaf, which no mortal can learn,—
Oh, there never was plant like the Irish hill Fern!

Oh, the Fern! the Fern!—the Irish hill Fern!—
That shelters the weary, or wild roe, or kern.
Through the glens of Kilcoe rose a shout on the gale,
As the Saxons rushed forth, in their wrath, from the Pale,
With bandog and blood-hound, all savage to see,
To hunt through Clunealla the wild Rapparee!
Hark! a cry from yon dell on the startled ear rings,
And forth from the wood the young fugitive springs.

Through the copse, o'er the bog, and, oh saints be his guide!
His fleet step now falters—there's blood on his side!
Yet onward he strains, climbs the cliff, fords the stream,
And sinks on the hill-top 'mid bracken leaves green,
And thick o'er his brow are their fresh clusters piled,
And they cover his form, as a mother her child;
And the Saxon is baffled!—they never discern
Where it shelters and saves him—the Irish hill Fern!

Oh, the Fern! the Fern!—the Irish hill Fern!—
That pours a wild keen o'er the hero's grey cairn;
Go, hear it at midnight, when stars are all out,
And the wind o'er the hill-side is moaning about,
With a rustle and stir, and a low wailing tone

That thrills through the heart with its whispering lone;
And ponder its meaning, when haply you stray
Where the halls of the stranger in ruin decay.

With night-owls for warders, the goshawk for guest,
And their dais of honour by cattle-hoofs prest,
With its fosse choked with rushes, and spider-webs flung
Over walls where the marchmen their red weapons hung,
With a curse on their name, and a sigh for the hour
That tarries so long—look! what waves on the tower?
With an omen and sign, and an augury stern,
'Tis the Green Flag of Time!—'tis the Irish hill Fern!

JOSEPH SHERIDAN LE FANU (1814–1873)
Le Fanu was a Dublin-born journalist and Gothic novelist.

A Drunkard's Address to a Bottle of Whiskey

From what dripping cell, through what fairy glen,
Where 'mid old rocks and ruins the fox makes his den;
Over what lonesome mountain,
              Acushla machree!
            Where gauger never has trod,
            Sweet as the flowery sod,
            Wild as the breath
            Of the breeze on the heath,
And sparklin' all o'er like the moon-lighted fountain,
            Are you come to me—
            Sorrowful me?

            Dancing—inspirin'—
            My wild blood firin';
            Oh! terrible glory—
            Oh! beautiful siren—
            Come, tell the old story—
Come light up my fancy, and open my heart.
            Oh! beautiful ruin—
            My life—my undoin'—
            Soft and fierce as a pantheress,
            Dream of my longing and wreck of my soul,
I never knew love till I loved you, enchantheress!
    At first, when I knew you, 'twas only flirtation,

The touch of a lip and the flash of an eye;
   But 'tis different now—'tis desperation!
        I worship before you,
        I curse and adore you,
And without you I'd die.

          Wirrasthrue!
        I wish 'twas again
        The happy time when
        I cared little about you,
        Could do well without you,
        But would just laugh and view you;
        'Tis little I knew you!
        Oh! terrible darlin',
        How have you sought me,
        Enchanted, and caught me?
        See, now, where you've brought me—
To sleep by the road-side, and dress out in rags,
        Think how you found me;
        Dreams come around me—
The dew of my childhood, and life's morning beam;
Now I sleep by the roadside, a wretch all in rags.
My heart that sang merrily when I was young,
   Swells up like a billow and bursts in despair;
And the wreck of my hopes on sweet memory flung,
   And cries on the air,
Are all that is left of the dream.

          Wirrasthrue!
        My father and mother,
        The priest, and my brother—
        Not a one has a good word for you.
But I can't part you, darling, their preachin's all vain;
   You'll burn in my heart till these thin pulses stop,
And the wild cup of life in your fragrance I'll drain
   To the last brilliant drop.

        Then oblivion will cover
        The shame that is over,
The brain that was mad, and the heart that was sore.
        Then, beautiful witch,
        I'll be found—in a ditch,
With your kiss on my cold lips, and never rise more.

AUBREY DE VERE (1814–1902)
De Vere, who was born in County Limerick,
was a scholar at University College, Dublin.

The New Race

O ye who have vanquished the land and retain it,
    How little ye know what ye miss of delight!
There are worlds in her heart—could ye seek it or gain it—
    That would clothe a true noble with glory and might.

What is she, this Isle which ye trample and ravage,
    Which ye plough with oppression, and reap with the sword,
But a harp, never strung, in the hall of a savage,
    Or a fair wife embraced by a husband abhorred?

The chiefs of the Gael were the people embodied;
    The chiefs were the blossoms, the people the root!
Their conquerors, the Normans, high-souled and high-blooded,
    Grew Irish at last from the scalp to the foot.

And ye!—ye are hirelings and satraps, not nobles!
    Your slaves, they detest you; your masters, they scorn!
The river lives on—but the sun-painted bubbles
    Pass quick, to the rapids insensibly borne.

MICHAEL JOSEPH BARRY (1817–1889)
Barry was a lawyer, writer, and editor, born in Cork.

Hymn of Freedom

God of Peace! before thee,
    Peaceful, here we kneel,
Humbly to implore thee
    For a nation's weal.
Calm her sons' dissensions,
    Bid their discord cease,
End their mad contentions—
    Hear us, God of Peace!

God of Love! low bending,
    To thy throne we turn;

Let thy rays, descending,
  Through our island burn.
Let no strife divide us,
  But, from Heaven above,
Look on us and guide us—
  Hear us, God of Love!

God of Battles! aid us;
  Let no despot's might
Trample or degrade us,
  Seeking this our right!
Arm us for the danger;
  Keep all craven fear
To our breasts a stranger—
  God of Battles! hear.

God of Right! preserve us
  Just—as we are strong;
Let no passion swerve us
  To one act of wrong;
Let no thought unholy
  Come our cause to blight;
Thus we pray thee, lowly—
  Hear us, God of Right!

God of Vengeance! smite us
  With thy shaft sublime,
If one bond unite us
  Forged in fraud or crime!
But if, humbly kneeling,
  We implore thine ear,
For our rights appealing—
  God of Nations! hear.

DENIS FLORENCE McCARTHY (1817–1882)

McCarthy was a lawyer, poet, and professor, born in Dublin.

The Irish Wolf-Hound

His stature tall, his body long,
  His back like night, his breast like snow,
His fore-leg pillar-like and strong,
  His hind-leg like a bended bow;

Rough curling hair, head long and thin,
　His ear a leaf so small and round;
Not Bran, the favourite dog of Finn,
　Could rival John MacDonnell's hound.

As fly the shadows o'er the grass,
　He flies with step as light and sure,
He hunts the wolf through Tostan pass,
　And starts the deer by Lisanoure.
The music of the Sabbath bells,
　O Con! has not a sweeter sound
Than when along the valley swells
　The cry of John MacDonnell's hound.

DION BOUCICAULT (1822–1890)
Boucicault was a Dublin-born playwright, actor, and theatre manager.

The Wearing of the Green
There are many versions of this song; Boucicault's is among the most popular.

O Paddy dear, and did you hear the news that's going round?
The shamrock is forbid by law to grow on Irish ground;
St. Patrick's day no more we'll keep, his colours can't be seen,
For there's a bloody law again' the wearing of the green.
I met with Napper Tandy, and he took me by the hand,
And he said, "How's poor old Ireland, and how does she stand?"
She's the most distressful country that ever yet was seen,
They are hanging men and women for the wearing of the green.

Then since the colour we must wear is England's cruel red,
Sure Ireland's sons will ne'er forget the blood that they have shed.
You may take the shamrock from your hat and cast it on the sod,
But 'twill take root and flourish there, though under foot 'tis trod.
When law can stop the blades of grass from growing as they grow,
And when the leaves in summer-time their verdure dare not show,
Then I will change the colour that I wear in my caubeen,
But till that day, please God, I'll stick to wearing of the green.

But if at last our colour should be torn from Ireland's heart,
Her sons with shame and sorrow from the dear old isle will part;
I've heard a whisper of a country that lies beyond the sea,
Where rich and poor stand equal in the light of freedom's day.
O Erin, must we leave you, driven by a tyrant's hand?

Must we ask a mother's blessing from a strange and distant land?
Where the cruel cross of England shall nevermore be seen,
And where, please God, we'll live and die still wearing of the green.

I'm Very Happy Where I Am: A Peasant Woman's Song, 1864

"A few days ago," wrote Boucicault, "I stood on the North Wall and watched the emigrants embarking for the Far West, as I have often stood on the quays of New York to see them arrive in America. While chewing the cud of many sweet and bitter fancies over this sad review, and picturing to myself the fate of each group as it passed, a chord in the old harp, which every Irishman wears in his breast, twanged in a minor key, and I heard a young Irish wife in the backwoods of Ohio singing this strain."

> I'm very happy where I am,
>   Far across the say,
> I'm very happy far from home,
>   In North Amerikay.
>
> It's lonely in the night, when Pat
>   Is sleeping by my side,
> I lie awake, and no one knows
>   The big tears that I've cried;
>
> For a little voice still calls me back
>   To my far, far counthrie,
> And nobody can hear it spake,
>   O! nobody but me.
>
> There is a little spot of ground
>   Behind the chapel wall,
> It's nothing but a tiny mound,
>   Without a stone at all;
>
> It rises like my heart just now,
>   It makes a dawny hill;
> It's from below the voice comes out,
>   I cannot keep it still.
>
> O! little Voice; ye call me back
>   To my far, far counthrie,
> And nobody can hear ye spake,
>   O! nobody but me.

THOMAS CAULFIELD IRWIN (1823–1892)

Irwin was a journalist and poet born in County Down.

The Potato-Digger's Song

Come, Connal, acushla, turn the clay,
    And show the lumpers the light, gossoon;
For we must toil this autumn day,
    With heaven's help till rise of the moon.
Our corn is stocked, our hay secure,
    Thank God! and nothing, my boy, remains,
But to pile the potatoes safe on the floor
    Before the coming November rains.
The peasant's mine is his harvest still;
So now, my lad, let's dig with a will;—
        Work hand and foot,
            Work spade and hand,
                Work spade and hand
                    Through the crumbly mould;
                    The blessed fruit
                        That grows at the root
                        Is the real gold
                        Of Ireland!

Och, I wish that Maurice and Mary dear
    Were singing beside us this soft day.
Of course they're far better off than here;
    But whether they're happier, who can say?
I've heard, when it's morn with us, 'tis night
    With them on the far Australian shore;—
Well! Heaven be about them with visions bright,
    And send them children and money galore.
With us there's many a mouth to fill,
And so, my boy, let's work with a will:—
        Work hand and foot, etc.

Ah, then, Paddy O'Reardan, you thundering Turk,
    Is it coorting you are in the blessed noon?
Come over here, Katty, and mind your work,
    Or I'll see if your mother can't change your tune.
Well—youth will be youth, as you know, Mike,
    Sixteen and twenty for each were meant;—
But Pat, in the name of the fairies, avic,
    Defer your proposals till after Lent;
And as Love in this country lives mostly still

On potatoes—dig, boy, dig with a will:—
    Work hand and foot, etc.

Down the bridle road the neighbours ride,
    Through the light ash shade, by the wheaten sheaves:
And the children sing on the mountain side,
    In the sweet blue smoke of the burning leaves.
As the great sun sets in glory furled,
    Faith, it's grand to think as I watch his face—
If he never sets on the English world,
    He never, lad, sets on the Irish race;
In the West, in the South, New Irelands still
Grow up in his light;—come, work with a will:—
    Work hand and foot, etc.

But look!—the round moon, yellow as corn,
    Comes up from the sea in the deep blue calm:
It scarcely seems a day since morn;
    Well—the heel of the day to you, ma'am!
God bless the moon; for many a night,
    As I restless lay on a troubled bed,
When rent was due—her quieting light
    Has flattered with dreams my poor old head;—
But see—the baskets remain to fill—
Come, girls, be alive—boys, dig with a will:—
    Work hand and foot, etc.

MARTIN MacDERMOTT (1823–1905)

In 1894, MacDermott edited The New Spirit of "The Nation":
Containing Songs and Ballads Published Since 1845.

Girl of the Red Mouth

Girl of the red mouth,
    Love me! Love me!
Girl of the red mouth,
    Love me!
'Tis by its curve, I know,
Love fashioneth his bow,
And bends it—ah, even so!
    Oh, girl of the red mouth, love me!

Girl of the blue eye,
    Love me! Love me!

Girl of the dew eye,
   Love me!
Worlds hang for lamps on high;
And thought's world lives in thy
Lustrous and tender eye—
   Oh, girl of the blue eye, love me!

Girl of the swan's neck,
   Love me! Love me!
Girl of the swan's neck,
   Love me!
As a marble Greek doth grow
To his steed's back of snow,
Thy white neck sits thy shoulder so,—
   Oh, girl of the swan's neck, love me!

Girl of the low voice,
   Love me! Love me!
Girl of the sweet voice,
   Love me!
Like the echo of a bell,—
Like the bubbling of a well—
Sweeter! Love within doth dwell,—
   Oh, girl of the low voice, love me!

WILLIAM ALLINGHAM (1824–1889)

*Known for his "countryside" poems, Allingham was born in Bally-
shannon, County Donegal. He became a literary figure in the Pre-
Raphaelite movement in London, where he died. His ashes were returned
to Ballyshannon and buried in the Church of Ireland cemetery there.*

Lovely Mary Donnelly

Oh, lovely Mary Donnelly, my joy, my only best!
If fifty girls were round you, I'd hardly see the rest;
Be what it may the time o' day, the place be where it will,
Sweet looks o' Mary Donnelly, they bloom before me still.

Her eyes like mountain water that's flowing on a rock,
How clear they are, how dark they are! they give me many a shock.
Red rowans warm in sunshine and wetted with a shower,
Could ne'er express the charming lip that has me in its power.

Her nose is straight and handsome, her eyebrows lifted up,
Her chin is very neat and pert, and smooth like a china cup,
Her hair's the brag of Ireland, so weighty and so fine;
It's rolling down upon her neck, and gather'd in a twine.

The dance o' last Whit-Monday night exceeded all before,
No pretty girl for miles about was missing from the floor;
But Mary kept the belt of love, and O but she was gay!
She danced a jig, she sung a song, that took my heart away.

When she stood up for dancing, her steps were so complete,
The music nearly killed itself to listen to her feet;
The fiddler moan'd his blindness, he heard her so much praised,
But bless'd his luck to not be deaf when once her voice she raised.

And evermore I'm whistling or lilting what you sung,
Your smile is always in my heart, your name beside my tongue;
But you've as many sweethearts as you'd count on both your hands,
And for myself there's not a thumb or little finger stands.

Oh, you're the flower o' womankind in country or in town;
The higher I exalt you, the lower I'm cast down.
If some great lord should come this way, and see your beauty bright,
And you to be his lady, I'd own it was but right.

O might we live together in a lofty palace hall,
Where joyful music rises, and where scarlet curtains fall!
O might we live together in a cottage mean and small,
With sods o' grass the only roof, and mud the only wall!

O lovely Mary Donnelly, your beauty's my distress,
It's far too beauteous to be mine, but I'll never wish it less.
The proudest place would fit your face, and I am poor and low;
But blessings be about you, dear, wherever you may go!

Four Ducks on a Pond

Four ducks on a pond,
A grass-bank beyond,
A blue sky of spring,
White clouds on the wing:
What a little thing
To remember for years—
To remember with tears!

A Dream

I heard the dogs howl in the moonlight night;
I went to the window to see the sight;
All the Dead that ever I knew
Going one by one and two by two.

On they pass'd, and on they pass'd;
Townsfellows all, from first to last;
Born in the moonlight of the lane,
Quench'd in the heavy shadow again.

Schoolmates, marching as when they play'd
At soldiers once—but now more staid;
Those were the strangest sight to me
Who were drown'd, I knew, in the awful sea.

Straight and handsome folk, bent and weak, too;
Some that I loved, and gasp'd to speak to;
Some but a day in their churchyard bed;
Some that I had not known were dead.

A long, long crowd—where each seem'd lonely,
Yet of them all there was one, one only,
Raised a head or look'd my way;
She linger'd a moment—she might not stay.

How long since I saw that fair pale face!
Ah! Mother dear! might I only place
My head on thy breast, a moment to rest,
While thy hand on my tearful cheek were prest!

On, on, a moving bridge they made
Across the moon-stream, from shade to shade,
Young and old, women and men;
Many long-forgot, but remember'd then,

And first there came a bitter laughter;
A sound of tears a moment after;
And then a music so lofty and gay,
That every morning, day by day,
I strive to recall it if I may.

The Winding Banks of Erne:
Or, The Emigrant's Adieu to His Birthplace

Adieu to Belashanny!* where I was bred and born;
Go where I may I'll think of you, as sure as night and morn;
The kindly spot, the friendly town, where everyone is known,
And not a face in all the place but partly seems my own;
There's not a house or window, there's not a field or hill,
But east or west, in foreign lands, I'll recollect them still;
I leave my warm heart with you, though my back I'm forced to turn—
So adieu to Belashanny and the winding banks of Erne!

No more on pleasant evenings we'll saunter down the Mall,
When the trout is rising to the fly, the salmon to the fall.
The boat comes straining on her net, and heavily she creeps,
Cast off, cast off—she feels the oars, and to her berth she sweeps;
Now fore and aft keep hauling, and gathering up the clew,
Till a silver wave of salmon rolls in among the crew.
Then they may sit with pipes alit, and many a joke and "yarn":—
Adieu to Belashanny and the winding banks of Erne!

The music of the waterfall, the mirror of the tide,
When all the green-hill'd harbour is full from side to side,
From Portnasun to Bulliebawns, and round the Abbey Bay,
From rocky Inis Saimer to Coolnargit sandhills gray;
While far upon the southern line, to guard it like a wall,
The Leitrim mountains clothed in blue gaze calmly over all,
And watch the ship sail up or down, the red flag at her stern;—
Adieu to these, adieu to all the winding banks of Erne!

Farewell to you, Kildoney lads, and them that pull an oar,
A lugsail set, or haul a net, from the Point to Mullaghmore;
From Killybegs to bold Slieve League, that ocean-mountain steep,
Six hundred yards in air aloft, six hundred in the deep;
From Dooran to the Fairy Bridge, and round by Tullen strand,
Level and long, and white with waves, where gull and curlew stand;
Head out to sea, when on your lee the breakers you discern!—
Adieu to all the billowy coast and winding banks of Erne!

Farewell Coolmore—Bundoran! and your summer crowds that run
From inland homes to see with joy th' Atlantic-setting sun;
To breathe the buoyant salted air, and sport among the waves;
To gather shells on sandy beach, and tempt the gloomy caves;
To watch the flowing, ebbing tide, the boats, the crabs, the fish;

*Vernacular and more correct name of the town usually called "Ballyshannon."—
H. Halliday Sparling.

Young men and maids to meet and smile, and form a tender wish;
The sick and old in search of health, for all things have their turn—
And I must quit my native shore and the winding banks of Erne!

Farewell to every white cascade from the Harbour to Belleek,
And every pool where fins may rest, and ivy-shaded creek;
The sloping fields, the lofty rocks, where ash and holly grow,
The one split yew-tree gazing on the curving flood below;
The Lough that winds through islands under Turaw mountain green;
And Castle Caldwell's stretching woods, with tranquil bays between;
And Breesie Hill, and many a pond among the heath and fern;—
For I must say adieu—adieu to the winding banks of Erne!

The thrush will call through Camlin groves the livelong summer day;
The waters run by mossy cliff, and banks with wild flowers gay;
The girls will bring their work and sing beneath a twisted thorn,
Or stray with sweethearts down the path among the growing corn;
Along the riverside they go, where I have often been,—
O never shall I see again the happy days I've seen!
A thousand chances are to one I never may return,—
Adieu to Belashanny and the winding banks of Erne!

Adieu to evening dances, when merry neighbours meet,
And the fiddle says to boys and girls, "Get up and shake your feet!"
To *seanachas** and wise old talk of Erin's days gone by—
Who trench'd the rath on such a hill, and where the bones may lie
Of saint or king or warrior chief; with tales of fairy power,
And tender ditties sweetly sung to pass the twilight hour.
The mournful song of exile is now for me to learn—
Adieu, my dear companions on the winding banks of Erne!

Now measure from the Commons down to each end of the Purt,
Round the Abbey, Moy, and Knather,—I wish no one any hurt;
The Main Street, Back Street, College Lane, the Mall, and Portnasun,
If any foes of mine are there, I pardon every one.
I hope that man and womankind will do the same by me;
For my heart is sore and heavy at voyaging the sea.
My loving friends I'll bear in mind, and often fondly turn
To think of Belashanny and the winding banks of Erne.

If ever I'm a money'd man, I mean, please God, to cast
My golden anchor in the place where youthful years were past;
Tho' heads that now are black and brown must meanwhile gather gray,
New faces rise by every hearth and old ones drop away—
Yet dearer still that Irish hill than all the world beside;

*Pronounced "Shanachas": history, genealogy, old stories.—*H. Halliday Sparling.*

It's home, sweet home, where'er I roam, through lands and waters wide.
And if the Lord allows me, I surely will return
To my native Belashanny and the winding banks of Erne.

THOMAS D'ARCY M'GEE (1821–1868)

*Born in Carlingford, M'gee emigrated to the U.S. at age sev-
enteen, and edited* The Boston Pilot. *In 1857, he moved to
Montreal and became a member of the Canadian parliament.*

Home Thoughts

If Will had wings,
    How fast I'd flee,
To the home of my heart
    O'er the seething sea!
If Wishes were power,
    If Words were spells,
I'd be this hour
    Where my own love dwells.

My own love dwells
    In the storied land,
Where the Holy Wells
    Sleep in yellow sand;
And the emerald lustre
    Of Paradise beams,
Over homes that cluster
    Round singing streams.

I, sighing, alas!
    Exist alone;
My youth is as grass
    On an unsunned stone;
Bright to the eye,
    But unfelt below,
As sunbeams that lie
    Over Arctic snow.

My heart is a lamp
    That love must relight,
Or the world's fire-damp
    Will quench it quite;
In the breast of my dear,
    My life-tide springs—

Oh! I'd hurry home here,
   If Will had wings.

For she never was weary
   Of blessing me,
When morn rose dreary
   On thatch and tree;
She evermore chanted
   Her song of Faith,
When darkness daunted
   On hill and heath.

If Will had wings,
   How fast I'd flee
To the home of my heart
   O'er the seething sea!
If Wishes were power,
   If Words were spells,
I'd be this hour
   Where my own love dwells.

CHARLES JOSEPH KICKHAM (1830–1882)

*Born in County Tipperary, Kickham suffered imprisonment
during the revolutionary Fenian movement of the 1840s.*

The Irish Peasant Girl

She lived beside the Anner,
At the foot of Slievna-man,
A gentle peasant girl,
With mild eyes like the dawn;
Her lips were dewy rosebuds;
Her teeth of pearls rare;
And a snow-drift 'neath a beechen bough
Her neck and nut-brown hair.

How pleasant 'twas to meet her
On Sunday, when the bell
Was filling with its mellow tones
Lone wood and grassy dell
And when at eve young maidens
Strayed the river bank along,
The widow's brown-haired daughter
Was loveliest of the throng.

O brave, brave Irish girls—
We well may call you brave!—
Sure the least of all your perils
Is the stormy ocean wave,
When you leave our quiet valleys,
And cross the Atlantic's foam,
To hoard your hard-won earnings
For the helpless ones at home.

"Write word to my own dear mother—
Say, we'll meet with God above;
And tell my little brothers
I send them all my love;
May the angels ever guard them,
Is their dying sister's prayer"—
And folded in a letter
Was a braid of nut-brown hair.

Ah, cold and well-nigh callous,
This weary heart has grown
For thy helpless fate, dear Ireland,
And for sorrows of my own;
Yet a tear my eye will moisten,
When by Anner side I stray,
For the lily of the mountain foot
That withered far away.

JOHN TODHUNTER (1839–1916)

Todhunter was a doctor, poet, and playwright, born in Dublin.

Song

Bring from the craggy haunts of birch and pine,
    Thou wild wind, bring
Keen forest odours from that realm of thine,
    Upon thy wing!

Oh! wind, Oh! mighty, melancholy wind,
    Blow through me, blow!
Thou blowest forgotten things into my mind,
    From long ago.

EMILY LAWLESS (1845–1913)

Lawless was a novelist and poet, born in County Kildare.

In Spain

Your sky is a hard and a dazzling blue,
Your earth and sands are a dazzling gold,
And gold or blue is the proper hue,
You say for a swordsman bold.

In the land I have left the skies are cold,
The earth is green, the rocks are bare,
Yet the devil may hold all your blue and your gold
Were I only once back there!

G. F. SAVAGE-ARMSTRONG (1845–1906)

George Francis Savage-Armstrong was a poet and play-
wright, and professor of English at Trinity College, Dublin.

The Wee Lassie's First Luve

A cannae hear his name an' hide
  My thought wi' ony art;
A cannae see him come, an' calm
  The flitterin' uv my heart;
It's pain tae meet him when A walk,
  Or meet him nae ava;
A wish him aye to come tae me,
  A wish him aye awa'.

A dinnae ken what's wrang wi' me;
  A'm vixed, A kennae why;
A cannae talk, A cannae wark;
  My min's a' ganged agley;
A say sich foolish thin's at whiles
  My face is scorch'd wi' pain . . .
O, let them lave me tae mysel'!
    A jist wud be alane.

A'm nae sae tall as Elsie Barnes,
  A hae nae een like May's,
Yit aft he turns frae May tae me,
  An' ne'er wi' Elsie strays.

A cannae thole tae see him laugh
   Wi' Grace or Rose or Jean,
An' yit he's standin' nigh my side
   Mair aft than ony ane.

He's aye sae coorteous, kin' an' free
   Wi' mon an' lass an' chiel',
Mayhap he cares nae mair fur me
   Than jist tae wish me weel . . .
But ah, the kin'ness uv his voice
   An' ah, his dark blue ee'
An' ah, his face an' coortly grace . . .
   A think A jist cud dee.

CHARLOTTE GRACE O'BRIEN (1845–1909)
O'Brien was a novelist and poet, born in Cahirmoyle.

The River

Poor Mick was trotting on to the town.
   The side car under him going;
He looked on the water, swollen and brown,
   He looked on the river flowing.

The day was drear and heavy and dank,
   A sleety wind was blowing,
And the river, creeping up over the bank,
   Was into the roadside going.

Now, all that day till the night drew near,
   For the wind was bitterly blowing,
Poor Mick sat gossiping here and there,
   While the river was steadily flowing.

"And why would ye lave? 'Tis a cruel night;
   Oh, why should ye be going?
Bide ye here till the morning light,
   For the blackest wind is blowing!"

"The wife will be wanting her bread and tay
   And oil for to light her sewing—
Myself never minded the roughest day
   Or the blackest black wind blowing.

"Gi' alang, ould mare! get up out of that!
   For sure 'tis home we're going!"
He buttoned his coat and settled his hat,
   Nor thought of the river flowing.

But cold and drear and dark was the night,
   The sleety wind was blowing,
And where the road that morning was right
   The river's edge was flowing.

Movrone! for the childer; movrone! for the wife,
   They listen the north winds blowing.
Movrone! for the gasping, struggling life,
   Movrone! for the river flowing.

The morrow's morn saw the trembling mare,
   Saw the river muddily flowing,
Saw boys and men seeking here and there,
   Though the soft south winds were blowing.

Oh! the early sun is fair to see,
   And the winter 'll soon be going,
But deep and dank and dark lies he,
   Though the sweet south winds are blowing.

ALFRED PERCEVAL GRAVES (1846–1931)
*This Dublin-born editor, poet, and translator
was also the father of the poet Robert Graves.*

The Song of the Ghost

When all were dreaming but Pastheen Power,
A light came streaming beneath her bower,
A heavy foot at her door delayed,
A heavy hand on the latch was laid.

"Now who dare venture at this dark hour,
Unbid to enter my maiden bower?"
"Dear Pastheen, open the door to me,
And your true lover you'll surely see."

"My own true lover, so tall and brave,
Lives exiled over the angry wave."
"Your true love's body lies on the bier,
His faithful spirit is with you here."

"His look was cheerful, his voice was gay:
Your speech is fearful, your look is gray;
And sad and sunken your eye of blue,
But Patrick, Patrick, alas 'tis you."

Ere dawn was breaking she heard below
The two cocks shaking their wings to crow.
"O hush you, hush you, both red and gray,
Or you will hurry my love away."

"O hush your crowing both gray and red
Or he'll be going to join the dead;
O cease from calling his ghost to the mould,
And I'll come crowning your combs with gold."

When all were dreaming but Pastheen Power,
A light went streaming from out her bower,
And on the morrow when they awoke,
They knew that sorrow her heart had broke.

The Irish Spinning-Wheel

Show me a sight
Bates for delight
An ould Irish wheel wid a young Irish girl at it.
Oh no!
Nothing you'll show
Aquals her sittin' an' takin' a twirl at it.

Look at her there—
Night in her hair,
The blue ray of day from her eye laughin' out on us!
Faix, an' a foot,
Perfect of cut,
Peepin' to put an end to all doubt in us.

That there's a sight
Bates for delight
An ould Irish wheel wid a young Irish girl at it—
Oh no!
Nothin' you'll show
Aquals her sittin' an' takin' a twirl at it.

See! the lamb's wool
Turns coarse an' dull
By them soft, beautiful weeshy white hands of her.

Down goes her heel,
Roun' runs the wheel,
Purrin' wid pleasure to take the commands of her.

Then show me a sight
Bates for delight
An ould Irish wheel wid a young Irish girl at it.
Oh no!
Nothin' you'll show
Aquals her sittin' an' takin' a twirl at it.

Talk of Three Fates,
Seated on sates,
Spinnin' and shearin' away till they've done for me!
You may want three
For your massacree,
But one Fate for me, boys—and only the one for me!

And isn't that fate
Pictured complate—
An ould Irish wheel with a young Irish girl at it?
Oh no!
Nothin' you'll show
Aquals her sittin' an' takin' a twirl at it.

FRANCIS A. FAHY (1854–1935)

*Fahy was a poet and songwriter, born in County Galway. He
achieved prominence in the Irish Literary Revival in London,
where he hobnobbed with the likes of G. B. Shaw and W. B. Yeats.*

Little Mary Cassidy

Oh, 'tis little Mary Cassidy's the cause of all my misery,
  And the raison that I am not now the boy I used to be;
Oh, she bates the beauties all that we read about in history,
  And sure half the country-side is as hot for her as me.
Travel Ireland up and down, hill, village, vale and town—
  Fairer than the Cailin Donn, you're looking for in vain;
Oh, I'd rather live in poverty with little Mary Cassidy
  Than emperor, without her, be of Germany or Spain.

'Twas at the dance at Darmody's that first I caught a sight of her,
  And heard her sing the "Droighnean Donn," till tears came in my
    eyes,

And ever since that blessed hour I'm dreaming day and night of her;
 The devil a wink of sleep at all I get from bed to rise.
Cheeks like the rose in June, song like the lark in tune,
 Working, resting, night or noon, she never leaves my mind;
Oh, till singing by my cabin fire sits little Mary Cassidy,
 'Tis little aise or happiness I'm sure I'll ever find.

What is wealth, what is fame, what is all that people fight about
 To a kind word from her lips or a love-glance from her eye?
Oh, though troubles throng my breast, sure they'd soon go to the right-
 about
 If I thought the curly head of her would rest there by and by.
Take all I own today, kith, kin, and care away,
 Ship them all across the say, or to the frozen zone:
Lave me an orphan bare—but lave me Mary Cassidy,
 I never would feel lonesome with the two of us alone.

OSCAR WILDE (1854–1900)
The great playwright and wit published poetry before becoming renowned.

Requiescat

Tread lightly, she is near
 Under the snow,
Speak gently, she can hear
 The daisies grow.

All her bright golden hair
 Tarnished with rust,
She that was young and fair
 Fallen to dust.

Lily-like, white as snow,
 She hardly knew
She was a woman, so
 Sweetly she grew.

Coffin-board, heavy stone,
 Lie on her breast,
I vex my heart alone,
 She is at rest.

Peace, Peace, she cannot hear
    Lyre or sonnet,
All my life's buried here,
    Heap earth upon it.

T. W. ROLLESTON (1857–1920)

Born in Shinrone, Thomas William Rolleston was a scholar and translator of German. Of the poem that follows he wrote, "Ruraidh O'Conchobhar, last king of Ireland, died and was buried in the monastery of St. Fechin at Cong, where his grave is still shown in that most beautiful and pathetic of Irish ruins."

The Grave of Rury

Clear as air, the western waters
evermore their sweet, unchanging song
Murmur in their stony channels
round O'Conor's sepulchre in Cong.

Crownless, hopeless, here he lingered;
year on year went by him like a dream,
While the far-off roar of conquest
murmured faintly like the singing stream.

Here he died, and here they tombed him
men of Fechin, chanting round his grave.
Did they know, ah! did they know it,
what they buried by the babbling wave?

Now above the sleep of Rury
holy things and great have passed away;
Stone by stone the stately Abbey
falls and fades in passionless decay.

Darkly grows the quiet ivy,
pale the broken arches glimmer through;
Dark upon the cloister-garden
dreams the shadow of the ancient yew.

Through the roofless aisles the verdure
flows, the meadow-sweet and fox-glove bloom.
Earth, the mother and consoler,
winds soft arms about the lonely tomb.

Peace and holy gloom possess him,
last of Gaelic monarchs of the Gael,

Slumbering by the young, eternal
river-voices of the western vale.

SIDNEY ROYSE LYSAGHT (1860–1941)

Lysaght was a poet and playwright, born in County Cork.

The Penalty of Love

If love should count you worthy, and should deign
    One day to seek your door and be your guest,
    Pause! ere you draw the bolt and bid him rest,
If in your old content you would remain.
For not alone he enters: in his train
    Are angels of the mists, the lonely quest,
    Dreams of the unfulfilled and unpossessed.
And sorrow, and life's immemorial pain.

He wakes desires you never may forget,
    He shows you stars you never saw before,
    He makes you share with him for evermore,
The burden of the world's divine regret.
How wise were you to open not!—and yet,
    How poor if you should turn him from the door.

WILLIAM BUTLER YEATS (1865–1939)

Generally regarded as Ireland's greatest poet, Yeats was born in Dublin, and helped establish worldwide admiration for Irish literature.

Down by the Salley Gardens

Down by the salley* gardens my love and I did meet;
She passed the salley gardens with little snow-white feet.
She bid me take love easy, as the leaves grow on the tree;
But I, being young and foolish, with her would not agree.

In a field by the river my love and I did stand,
And on my leaning shoulder she laid her snow-white hand.
She bid me take life easy, as the grass grows on the weirs;
But I was young and foolish, and now am full of tears.

*Willow.

The Ballad of Father Gilligan

The old priest, Peter Gilligan,
Was weary night and day;
For half his flock were in their beds,
Or under green sods lay.

Once, while he nodded on a chair,
At the moth-hour of eve,
Another poor man sent for him,
And he began to grieve.

"I have no rest, nor joy, nor peace,
For people die and die";
And after cried he, "God forgive!
My body spake, not I!"

He knelt, and leaning on the chair
He prayed and fell asleep,
And the moth-hour went from the fields,
And stars began to peep.

They slowly into millions grew,
And leaves shook in the wind,
And God covered the world with shade,
And whispered to mankind.

Upon the time of sparrow chirp
When the moths come once more,
The old priest, Peter Gilligan,
Stood upright on the floor.

"Mavrone, mavrone! the man has died,
While I slept on the chair."
He roused his horse out of its sleep,
And rode with little care.

He rode now as he never rode,
By rocky lane and fen;
The sick man's wife opened the door:
"Father! you come again."

"And is the poor man dead?" he cried.
"He died an hour ago."
The old priest, Peter Gilligan,
In grief swayed to and fro.

"When you were gone, he turned and died
As merry as a bird."

The old priest, Peter Gilligan,
He knelt him at that word.

"He who hath made the night of stars
For souls who tire and bleed,
Sent one of His great angels down
To help me in my need.

"He who is wrapped in purple robes,
With planets in His care,
Had pity on the least of things
Asleep upon a chair."

To Ireland in the Coming Times

Know, that I would accounted be
True brother of that company,
Who sang to sweeten Ireland's wrong,
Ballad and story, rann* and song;
Nor be I any less of them,
Because the red-rose-bordered hem
Of her, whose history began
Before God made the angelic clan,
Trails all about the written page;
For in the world's first blossoming age
The light fall of her flying feet
Made Ireland's heart begin to beat;
And still the starry candles flare
To help her light foot here and there;
And still the thoughts of Ireland brood
Upon her holy quietude.

Nor may I less be counted one
With Davis, Mangan, Ferguson,
Because to him, who ponders well,
My rhymes more than their rhyming tell
Of the dim wisdoms old and deep,
That God gives unto man in sleep.
For the elemental beings go
About my table to and fro.
In flood and fire and clay and wind,
They huddle from man's pondering mind;
Yet he who treads in austere ways
May surely meet their ancient gaze.

*Verse.

Man ever journeys on with them
After the red-rose-bordered hem.
Ah, faeries, dancing under the moon,
A Druid land, a Druid tune!

While still I may, I write for you
The love I lived, the dream I knew.
From our birthday, until we die,
Is but the winking of an eye;
And we, our singing and our love,
The mariners of night above,
And all the wizard things that go
About my table to and fro,
Are passing on to where may be,
In truth's consuming ecstasy
No place for love and dream at all;
For God goes by with white foot-fall.
I cast my heart into my rhymes,
That you, in the dim coming times,
May know how my heart went with them
After the red-rose-bordered hem.

The Host of the Air

O'Driscoll drove with a song
The wild duck and the drake
From the tall and the tufted reeds
Of the drear Hart Lake.

And he saw how the reeds grew dark
At the coming of night tide,
And dreamed of the long dim hair
Of Bridget his bride.

He heard while he sang and dreamed
A piper piping away,
And never was piping so sad,
And never was piping so gay.

And he saw young men and young girls
Who danced on a level place,
And Bridget his bride among them,
With a sad and a gay face.

The dancers crowded about him,
And many a sweet thing said,

And a young man brought him red wine
And a young girl white bread.

But Bridget drew him by the sleeve,
Away from the merry bands,
To old men playing at cards
With a twinkling of ancient hands.

The bread and the wine had a doom,
For these were the host of the air;
He sat and played in a dream
Of her long dim hair.

He played with the merry old men
And thought not of evil chance,
Until one bore Bridget his bride
Away from the merry dance.

He bore her away in his arms,
The handsomest young man there,
And his neck and his breast and his arms
Were drowned in her long dim hair.

O'Driscoll scattered the cards
And out of his dream awoke:
Old men and young men and young girls
Were gone like a drifting smoke;

But he heard high up in the air
A piper piping away,
And never was piping so sad,
And never was piping so gay.

The Song of Wandering Aengus

I went out to the hazel wood,
   Because a fire was in my head,
And cut and peeled a hazel wand,
   And hooked a berry to a thread;
And when white moths were on the wing,
   And moth-like stars were flickering out,
I dropped the berry in a stream
   And caught a little silver trout.

When I had laid it on the floor
   I went to blow the fire a-flame,

But something rustled on the floor,
    And someone called me by my name:
It had become a glimmering girl
    With apple blossom in her hair
Who called me by my name and ran
    And faded through the brightening air.

Though I am old with wandering
    Through hollow lands and hilly lands,
I will find out where she has gone,
    And kiss her lips and take her hands;
And walk among long dappled grass,
    And pluck till time and times are done
The silver apples of the moon,
    The golden apples of the sun.

September 1913

What need you, being come to sense,
But fumble in a greasy till
And add the halfpence to the pence
And prayer to shivering prayer, until
You have dried the marrow from the bone?
For men were born to pray and save,
Romantic Ireland's dead and gone,
It's with O'Leary* in the grave.

Yet they were of a different kind,
The names that stilled your childish play,
They have gone about the world like wind,
But little time had they to pray
For whom the hangman's rope was spun,
And what, God help us, could they save?
Romantic Ireland's dead and gone,
It's with O'Leary in the grave.

Was it for this the wild geese spread
The grey wing upon every tide;
For this that all that blood was shed,
For this Edward Fitzgerald† died,
And Robert Emmet and Wolfe Tone,‡
All that delirium of the brave?

*John O'Leary (1830–1907), an Irish patriot and friend of Yeats's father.
†A member of the United Irishmen; he died in 1798 from wounds received during his arrest.
‡Founder of the United Irish Club; he committed suicide in prison, in 1798.

Romantic Ireland's dead and gone,
It's with O'Leary in the grave.

Yet could we turn the years again,
And call those exiles as they were,
In all their loneliness and pain,
You'd cry, "Some woman's yellow hair
Has maddened every mother's son":
They weighed so lightly what they gave,
But let them be, they're dead and gone,
They're with O'Leary in the grave.

In Memory of Major Robert Gregory

I

Now that we're almost settled in our house
I'll name the friends that cannot sup with us
Beside a fire of turf in th' ancient tower,
And having talked to some late hour
Climb up the narrow winding stair to bed:
Discoverers of forgotten truth
Or mere companions of my youth,
All, all are in my thoughts tonight being dead.

II

Always we'd have the new friend meet the old
And we are hurt if either friend seem cold,
And there is salt to lengthen out the smart
In the affections of our heart,
And quarrels are blown up upon that head;
But not a friend that I would bring
This night can set us quarrelling,
For all that come into my mind are dead.

III

Lionel Johnson comes the first to mind,
That loved his learning better than mankind,
Though courteous to the worst; much falling he
Brooded upon sanctity
Till all his Greek and Latin learning seemed
A long blast upon the horn that brought
A little nearer to his thought
A measureless consummation that he dreamed.

IV

And that enquiring man John Synge comes next
That dying chose the living world for text
And never could have rested in the tomb
But that, long travelling, he had come
Towards nightfall upon certain set apart
In a most desolate stony place,
Towards nightfall upon a race
Passionate and simple like his heart.

V

And then I think of old George Pollexfen,
In muscular youth well known to Mayo men
For horsemanship at meets or at racecourses,
That could have shown how purebred horses
And solid men, for all their passion, live
But as the outrageous stars incline
By opposition, square and trine;
Having grown sluggish and contemplative.

VI

They were my close companions many a year,
A portion of my mind and life, as it were,
And now their breathless faces seem to look
Out of some old picture-book;
I am accustomed to their lack of breath,
But not that my dear friend's dear son,
Our Sidney and our perfect man,
Could share in that discourtesy of death.

VII

For all things the delighted eye now sees
Were loved by him; the old storm-broken trees
That cast their shadows upon road and bridge;
The tower set on the stream's edge;
The ford where drinking cattle make a stir
Nightly, and startled by that sound
The water-hen must change her ground;
He might have been your heartiest welcomer.

VIII

When with the Galway foxhounds he would ride
From Castle Taylor to the Roxborough side
Or Esserkelly plain, few kept his pace;
At Mooneen he had leaped a place
So perilous that half the astonished meet
Had shut their eyes, and where was it
He rode a race without a bit?
And yet his mind outran the horses' feet.

IX

We dreamed that a great painter had been born
To cold Clare rock and Galway rock and thorn,
To that stern colour and that delicate line
That are our secret discipline
Wherein the gazing heart doubles her might.
Soldier, scholar, horseman, he,
And yet he had the intensity
To have published all to be a world's delight.

X

What other could so well have counselled us
In all lovely intricacies of a house
As he that practised or that understood
All work in metal or in wood,
In moulded plaster or in carven stone?
Soldier, scholar, horseman, he,
And all he did done perfectly
As though he had but that one trade alone.

XI

Some burn damp fagots, others may consume
The entire combustible world in one small room
As though dried straw, and if we turn about
The bare chimney is gone black out
Because the work had finished in that flare.
Soldier, scholar, horseman, he,
As 'twere all life's epitome.
What made us dream that he could comb grey hair?

XII

I had thought, seeing how bitter is that wind
That shakes the shutter, to have brought to mind
All those that manhood tried, or childhood loved
Or boyish intellect approved,
With some appropriate commentary on each;
Until imagination brought
A fitter welcome; but a thought
Of that late death took all my heart for speech.

An Irish Airman Foresees His Death

I know that I shall meet my fate
Somewhere among the clouds above;
Those that I fight I do not hate,
Those that I guard I do not love;
My country is Kiltartan Cross,
My countrymen Kiltartan's poor,
No likely end could bring them loss
Or leave them happier than before.
Nor law, nor duty bade me fight,
Nor public men, nor cheering crowds,
A lonely impulse of delight
Drove to this tumult in the clouds;
I balanced all, brought all to mind,
The years to come seemed waste of breath,
A waste of breath the years behind
In balance with this life, this death.

Easter 1916

I have met them at close of day
Coming with vivid faces
From counter or desk among grey
Eighteenth-century houses.
I have passed with a nod of the head
Or polite meaningless words,
Or have lingered awhile and said
Polite meaningless words,
And thought before I had done
Of a mocking tale or a gibe
To please a companion
Around the fire at the club,

Being certain that they and I
But lived where motley is worn:
All changed, changed utterly:
A terrible beauty is born.

That woman's days were spent
In ignorant good will,
Her nights in argument
Until her voice grew shrill.
What voice more sweet than hers
When young and beautiful,
She rode to harriers?
This man had kept a school
And rode our winged horse;
This other his helper and friend
Was coming into his force;
He might have won fame in the end,
So sensitive his nature seemed,
So daring and sweet his thought.
This other man I had dreamed
A drunken, vain-glorious lout.
He had done most bitter wrong
To some who are near my heart,
Yet I number him in the song;
He, too, has resigned his part
In the casual comedy;
He, too, has been changed in his turn,
Transformed utterly:
A terrible beauty is born.

Hearts with one purpose alone
Through summer and winter seem
Enchanted to a stone
To trouble the living stream.
The horse that comes from the road,
The rider, the birds that range
From cloud to tumbling cloud,
Minute by minute they change;
A shadow of cloud on the stream
Changes minute by minute;
A horse-hoof slides on the brim,
And a horse plashes within it
Where long-legged moor-hens dive,
And hens to moor-cocks call.
Minute by minute they live:
The stone's in the midst of all.

Too long a sacrifice
Can make a stone of the heart.
O when may it suffice?
That is heaven's part, our part
To murmur name upon name,
As a mother names her child
When sleep at last has come
On limbs that had run wild.
What is it but nightfall?
No, no, not night but death;
Was it needless death after all?
For England may keep faith
For all that is done and said.
We know their dream; enough
To know they dreamed and are dead;
And what if excess of love
Bewildered them till they died?
I write it out in a verse—
MacDonagh and MacBride
And Connolly and Pearse
Now and in time to be,
Wherever green is worn,
Are changed, changed utterly:
A terrible beauty is born.

The Second Coming

Turning and turning in the widening gyre
The falcon cannot hear the falconer;
Things fall apart; the centre cannot hold;
Mere anarchy is loosed upon the world,
The blood-dimmed tide is loosed, and everywhere
The ceremony of innocence is drowned;
The best lack all conviction, while the worst
Are full of passionate intensity.

Surely some revelation is at hand;
Surely the Second Coming is at hand.
The Second Coming! Hardly are those words out
When a vast image out of *Spiritus Mundi*
Troubles my sight: somewhere in sands of the desert
A shape with lion body and the head of a man,
A gaze blank and pitiless as the sun,
Is moving its slow thighs, while all about it
Reel shadows of the indignant desert birds.

The darkness drops again; but now I know
That twenty centuries of stony sleep
Were vexed to nightmare by a rocking cradle,
And what rough beast, its hour come round at last,
Slouches towards Bethlehem to be born?

MOIRA O'NEILL (1865–1955)

"Moira O'Neill" was the pen name of Nesta Shakespeare Higginson Skrine, who was born in County Antrim, and eventually settled in Canada after her marriage.

The Grand Match

Dennis was hearty when Dennis was young,
High was his step in the jig that he sprung,
He had the looks an' the sootherin' tongue,—
     An' he wanted a girl wid a fortune.

Nannie was grey-eyed, an' Nannie was tall,
Fair was the face hid inundher her shawl,
Troth! an' he liked her the best o' them all,—
     But she'd not a *traneen* to her fortune.

He be to look out for a likelier match,
So he married a girl that was counted a catch,
An' as ugly as need be, the dark little patch,—
     But that was a trifle, he tould her.

She brought him her good-lookin' gold to admire,
She brought him her good-lookin' cows to his byre,
But, far from good-lookin' she sat by his fire,—
     And paid him that "trifle" he tould her.

He met pretty Nan when a month had gone by,
An' he thought, like a fool, to get round her he'd try,
Wid a smile on her lip and a spark in her eye,
     She said, "How is the woman that owns ye?"

Och, never be tellin' the life that he's led!
Sure many's the night that he'll wish himself dead,
For the sake of two eyes in a pretty girl's head,—
     An' the tongue of the woman that owns him.

HERBERT TRENCH (1865–1923)

(Frederick) Herbert Trench was a poet who also
wrote for the theatre. He was born in County Cork.

Killary

When all her brothers in the house
    Were lying asleep, my love
Ran before me under the bend of boughs,
    Till we looked down from above
        On the long loch,
        On the brown loch,
        On the lone loch of Killary.

Together we ran down the copse
    And stood in the rain as close
As the birds that sleep in the soft tops
    Of the tree that comes and goes,
        When the morn moon,
        When the young moon,
        When the morn moon is on Killary!

In tremblings of the water chill
    Swans we saw preen their coat,
Biting their plumes, with stoop'd bill
    And quivering neck, afloat
        On the brown shade,
        On the deep shade,
        The shade of hills on Killary.

"Why pale, my beloved, now
    When the first light 'gins to beat?
No sun of autumn is rich as thou,
    And honey after thy feet
        Shall rise from the grass,
        From the wet of the grass,
        The brow of the grass over Killary!"

"My grief it is only that thou and I
    Must part, like swans of the flood
That rise up sorrowful into the sky;
    For one goes over the wood,
        And one oversea,
        And one oversea,
        And one oversea from Killary!

"Ah, the little raindrops that hang on the bough,
    Together they may run,
But never again shall I and thou
    Meet here in the morning sun . . .
        We shall meet no more,
        We must kiss no more,
        We shall meet no more by Killary!"

SUSAN L. MITCHELL (1866–1926)

*A poet and friend of A.E., Mitchell was born in County Sligo.
Amergin, the speaker of the following poem, was a judge and
poet in pre-Christian Ireland. Fragments of his poems survive.*

Amergin

I buzz in the dizzy fly, I crawl in the creeping things.
I croak in the frog's throat and fly on the bird's wings.

I play on the keys of the brain, a thought goes here, goes there;
Bird or beast it has bounds, but I am everywhere.

I dip in the pools of the rocks and the minnow plays with me.
Finned I am like a fish, and merry children are we.

At the dumb call of darkness I go to the ocean's side,
I stand on the docile beach and bridle the eager tide.

The fretted waters I hold in the hollow of my hand.
From my heart go fire and dew and the green and the brown land.

A.E. (1867–1935)

*A.E. was the pen name of the painter and mystical poet George
Russell. Sometimes known as the Irish William Blake, he was
revered by W. B. Yeats.*

Forgiveness

At dusk the window panes grew grey;
    The wet world vanished in the gloom;
The dim and silver end of day
    Scarce glimmered through the little room.

And all my sins were told; I said
　　Such things to her who knew not sin—
The sharp ache throbbing in my head,
　　The fever running high within—

I touched with pain her purity;
　　Sin's darker sense I could not bring;
My soul was black as night to me;
　　To her I was a wounded thing.

I needed love no words could say;
　　She drew me softly nigh her chair,
My head upon her knees to lay,
　　With cool hands that caressed my hair.

She sat with hands as if to bless,
　　And looked with grave, ethereal eyes;
Ensouled with ancient Quietness,
　　A gentle priestess of the Wise.

LIONEL JOHNSON (1867–1902)

*The son of an Irish army officer, Johnson was born in England,
but later became Catholic and a fervent Irish nationalist.*

The Red Wind

Red Wind from out the East:
　　Red Wind of blight and blood!
Ah, when wilt thou have ceased
　　Thy bitter, stormy flood?

Red Wind from over sea,
　　Scourging our lonely land!
What Angel loosened thee
　　Out of his iron hand?

Red Wind! whose word of might
　　Winged thee with wings of flame?
O fire of mournful night,
　　What is thy master's name?

Red Wind! who bade thee burn,
　　Branding our hearts? who bade
Thee on and never turn,
　　Till waste our souls were laid?

Red Wind! from out the West
  Pour Winds of Paradise:
Winds of eternal rest,
  That weary souls entice.

Wind of the East! Red Wind!
  Thou witherest the soft breath
Of Paradise the kind:
  Red Wind of burning death!

O Red Wind! hear God's voice:
  Hear thou, and fall, and cease.
Let Inisfail rejoice
  In her Hesperian peace.

JOHN MILLINGTON SYNGE (1871–1909)

The author of Ireland's most famous plays, including The
Playboy of the Western World, *was born near Dublin.*

Beg-Innish

Bring Kateen-beug and Maurya Jude
  To dance in Beg-Innish,
And when the lads (they're in Dunquin)
  Have sold their crabs and fish,
Wave fawny shawls and call them in,
And call the little girls who spin,
And seven weavers from Dunquin,
  To dance in Beg-Innish.

I'll play you jigs, and Maurice Kean,
  Where nets are laid to dry,
I've silken strings would draw a dance
  From girls are lame or shy;
Four strings I've brought from Spain and France
To make your long men skip and prance,
Till stars look out to see the dance
  Where nets are laid to dry.

We'll have no priest or peeler in
  To dance in Beg-Innish;
But we'll have drink from M'riarty Jim
  Rowed round while gannets fish,

A keg with porter to the brim,
That every lad may have his whim,
Till we up sails with M'riarty Jim
   And sail from Beg-Innish.

P. H. PEARSE (1879–1916)

*Padraic Henry Pearse, an activist, teacher and author, was executed
for his part in the 1916 uprising of the Irish Republican Brotherhood.*

The Wayfarer

The beauty of the world hath made me sad,
This beauty that will pass;
Sometimes my heart hath shaken with great joy
To see a leaping squirrel in a tree,
Or a red lady-bird upon a stalk,
Or little rabbits in a field at evening,
Lit by a slanting sun,
Or some green hill where shadows drifted by
Some quiet hill where mountainy man hath sown
And soon would reap; near to the gate of Heaven;
Or children with bare feet upon the sands
Of some ebbed sea, or playing on the streets
Of little towns in Connacht,
Things young and happy.
And then my heart hath told me:
These will pass,
Will pass and change, will die and be no more,
Things bright and green, things young and happy;
And I have gone upon my way
Sorrowful.

JOSEPH CAMPBELL (1879–1944)

A poet born in Belfast, Campbell later taught at Fordham University in New York.

The Old Woman

As a white candle
In a holy place,
So is the beauty
Of an agèd face.

As the spent radiance
Of the winter sun,
So is a woman
With her travail done.

Her brood gone from her
And her thoughts as still
As the waters
Under a ruined mill.

The Blind Man at the Fair

O to be blind!
To know the darkness that I know.
The stir I hear is empty wind,
The people idly come and go.

The sun is black, tho' warm and kind,
The horsemen ride, the streamers blow
Vainly in the fluky wind,
For all is darkness where I go.

The cattle bellow to their kind,
The mummers dance, the jugglers throw,
The thimble-rigger speaks his mind—
But all is darkness where I go.

I feel the touch of womankind,
Their dresses flow as white as snow;
But beauty is a withered rind
For all is darkness where I go.

Last night the moon of Lammas shined,
Rising high and setting low;
But light is nothing to the blind—
All, all is darkness where they go.

White roads I walk with vacant mind,
White cloud-shapes round me drifting slow,
White lilies waving in the wind—
And darkness everywhere I go.

The Hills of Cualann

In the youth of summer
The hills of Cualann
Are two golden horns,
Two breasts of childing,
Two tents of light

In the ancient winter
They are two rusted swords,
Two waves of darkness,
Two moons of ice.

WILLIAM DARA (c. 1880s–c. 1930s)

*The author's real name was William A. Byrne. He
lived a very secluded life as a Catholic college teacher.*

Song of a Turf-sod

Draw in your stools, good folk, for heating
    And gaze into mine eyes,
And see what sets the kind hearts beating,
    Where the lonesome cricket cries.

I was the broom and crookéd heather,
    I was the moss that grew,
But time has moulded us together
    Beneath the years of dew.

I kissed the elk's feet in my branches
    And trembled at his tramp
Ages before my purple ranches
    Were cut to make a clamp.

I heard the wild-ducks and the wild-geese
    Cackling about the lakes,
Where nothing now disturbs the mild peace
    The bog-rush meadow makes.

I show that winsome past is dying:
    Time hid it in my heart
Where, by a small stream's endless crying,
    I heard my youth depart.

I hold that past, but I will show it
    To the Irish faces only.
Folk, if you light me, you will know it,
    When the cricket makes you lonely!

Draw near, when round you chills are creeping
    From winds among the broom,
And shadows, from your shoulders leaping,
    Dance jigs about the room.

I have surprises, hid for showing,
    When by my light you start,
Watching the old, queer faces going
    Across my burning heart.

And while I doze in ashes piling,
    Perhaps yourself you'll see,
Through some old Gaelic gateway smiling
    In my antiquity.

PADRAIC COLUM (1881–1972)

*Colum was an author and editor who helped found the Abbey Theatre.
He was born in Longford, and lived much of his later life in the U.S.*

An Old Woman of the Roads

Oh, to have a little house,
    To own the hearth and stool and all—
The heaped-up sods upon the fire,
    The pile of turf against the wall!

To have a clock with weights and chains,
    And pendulum swinging up and down!
A dresser filled with shining delph,
    Speckled and white and blue and brown!

I could be busy all the day
    Clearing and sweeping hearth and floor,
And fixing on their shelf again
    My white and blue and speckled store.

I could be quiet there at night
  Beside the fire and by myself,
Sure of a bed, and loth to leave
  The ticking clock and shining delph.

Och! but I'm weary of mist and dark,
  And roads where there's never a house or bush,
And tired I am of bog and road,
  And the crying wind and the lonesome hush:

And I am praying to God on high,
  And I am praying Him night and day,
For a little house—a house of my own—
  Out of the wind's and the rain's way.

JAMES STEPHENS (1882–1950)
This Dublin-born author later became a radio broadcaster.

In the Poppy Field

Mad Patsy said, he said to me,
That every morning he could see
An angel walking on the sky;
Across the sunny skies of morn
He threw great handfuls far and nigh
Of poppy seed among the corn;
And then, he said, the angels run
To see the poppies in the sun.

A poppy is a devil weed,
I said to him—he disagreed:
He said the devil had no hand
In spreading flowers tall and fair
Through corn and rye and meadow land,
By garth and barrow everywhere:
The devil has not any flower,
But only money in his power.

And then he stretched out in the sun
And rolled upon his back for fun:
He kicked his legs and roared for joy
Because the sun was shining down,
He said he was a little boy
And would not work for any clown:
He ran and laughed behind a bee,
And danced for very ecstasy.

The Whisperer

The moon was round,
And as I walked along
There was no sound,
Save where the wind with long
Low hushes whispered to the ground
    A snatch of song.

No thought had I
Save that the moon was fair,
And fair the sky,
And God was everywhere.
I chanted as the wind went by
    A poet's prayer.

Then came a voice—
"Why is it that you praise
And thus rejoice,
O stranger to the ways
Of Providence? God has no choice
    In this sad maze.

"His law He laid
Down at the dread beginning,
When He made
The world and set it spinning,
And His casual hand betrayed
    Us into sinning.

"I fashion you,
And then for weal and woe,
My business through,
I care not how ye go,
Or struggle, win or lose, nor do
   I want to know.

"Is no appeal,
For I am far from sight,
And cannot feel
The rigour of your plight;
And if ye faint just when ye kneel,
   That, too, is right.

"Then do not sing,
O poet in the night,
That everything
Is beautiful and right.
What if some wind come now and fling
   At thee in spite?"

All in amaze
I listened to the tone
Mocking my praise:
And then I heard the groan
That old tormented nature did upraise
   From tree and stone.

And as I went
I heard it once again,
That harsh lament:
And fire came to my brain;
Deep anger unto me was lent
   To write this strain.

The Shell

And then I pressed the shell
Close to my ear
And listened well,
And straightway like a bell
Came low and clear
The slow, sad murmur of far distant seas,

Whipped by an icy breeze
Upon a shore
Wind-swept and desolate.
It was a sunless strand that never bore
The footprint of a man,
Nor felt the weight
Since time began
Of any human quality or stir
Save what the dreary winds and waves incur.
And in the hush of waters was the sound
Of pebbles rolling round,
For ever rolling with a hollow sound.
And bubbling sea-weeds as the waters go
Swish to and fro
Their long, cold tentacles of slimy grey.
There was no day,
Nor ever came a night
Setting the stars alight
To wonder at the moon:
Was twilight only and the frightened croon,
Smitten to whimpers, of the dreary wind
And waves that journeyed blind—
And then I loosed my ear—oh, it was sweet
To hear a cart go jolting down the street!

SHANE LESLIE (1885–1971)

The author of many books and novels, Leslie was born in County Monaghan.

Muckish Mountain (The Pig's Back)

Like a sleeping swine upon the skyline,
Muckish, thou art shadowed out,
Grubbing up the rubble of the ages
With your broken, granite snout.

Muckish, greatest pig in Ulster's oakwoods,
Littered out of rock and fire,
Deep you thrust your mottled flanks for cooling
Underneath the peaty mire.

Long before the Gael was young in Ireland,
You were ribbed and old and grey,
Muckish, you have long outstayed his staying,
You have seen him swept away.

Muckish, you will not forget the people
Of the laughing speech and eye,
They who gave you name of Pig-back-mountain
And the Heavens for a sty!

Alphabetical Index of Titles and First Lines

DOVER·THRIFT·EDITIONS

POETRY

A SHROPSHIRE LAD, A. E. Housman. 64pp. 26468-8 $1.00

LYRIC POEMS, John Keats. 80pp. 26871-3 $1.00

GUNGA DIN AND OTHER FAVORITE POEMS, Rudyard Kipling. 80pp. 26471-8 $1.00

THE CONGO AND OTHER POEMS, Vachel Lindsay. 96pp. 27272-9 $1.50

EVANGELINE AND OTHER POEMS, Henry Wadsworth Longfellow. 64pp. 28255-4 $1.00

FAVORITE POEMS, Henry Wadsworth Longfellow. 96pp. 27273-7 $1.00

"TO HIS COY MISTRESS" AND OTHER POEMS, Andrew Marvell. 64pp. 29544-3 $1.00

SPOON RIVER ANTHOLOGY, Edgar Lee Masters. 144pp. 27275-3 $1.50

RENASCENCE AND OTHER POEMS, Edna St. Vincent Millay. 64pp. (Available in U.S. only.) 26873-X $1.00

SELECTED POEMS, John Milton. 128pp. 27554-X $1.50

CIVIL WAR POETRY: An Anthology, Paul Negri (ed.). 128pp. 29883-3 $1.50

ENGLISH VICTORIAN POETRY: AN ANTHOLOGY, Paul Negri (ed.). 256pp. 40425-0 $2.00

GREAT SONNETS, Paul Negri (ed.). 96pp. 28052-7 $1.00

THE RAVEN AND OTHER FAVORITE POEMS, Edgar Allan Poe. 64pp. 26685-0 $1.00

ESSAY ON MAN AND OTHER POEMS, Alexander Pope. 128pp. 28053-5 $1.50

EARLY POEMS, Ezra Pound. 80pp. (Available in U.S. only.) 28745-9 $1.00

GREAT POEMS BY AMERICAN WOMEN: An Anthology, Susan L. Rattiner (ed.). 224pp. (Available in U.S. only.) 40164-2 $2.00

LITTLE ORPHANT ANNIE AND OTHER POEMS, James Whitcomb Riley. 80pp. 28260-0 $1.00

"MINIVER CHEEVY" AND OTHER POEMS, Edwin Arlington Robinson. 64pp. 28756-4 $1.00

GOBLIN MARKET AND OTHER POEMS, Christina Rossetti. 64pp. 28055-1 $1.00

CHICAGO POEMS, Carl Sandburg. 80pp. 28057-8 $1.00

THE SHOOTING OF DAN MCGREW AND OTHER POEMS, Robert Service. 96pp. (Available in U.S. only.) 27556-6 $1.50

COMPLETE SONNETS, William Shakespeare. 80pp. 26686-9 $1.00

SELECTED POEMS, Percy Bysshe Shelley. 128pp. 27558-2 $1.50

AFRICAN-AMERICAN POETRY: An Anthology, 1773–1930, Joan R. Sherman (ed.). 96pp. 29604-0 $1.00

100 BEST-LOVED POEMS, Philip Smith (ed.). 96pp. 28553-7 $1.00

NATIVE AMERICAN SONGS AND POEMS: An Anthology, Brian Swann (ed.). 64pp. 29450-1 $1.00

SELECTED POEMS, Alfred Lord Tennyson. 112pp. 27282-6 $1.50

AENEID, Vergil (Publius Vergilius Maro). 256pp. 28749-1 $2.00

CHRISTMAS CAROLS: COMPLETE VERSES, Shane Weller (ed.). 64pp. 27397-0 $1.00

GREAT LOVE POEMS, Shane Weller (ed.). 128pp. 27284-2 $1.00

CIVIL WAR POETRY AND PROSE, Walt Whitman. 96pp. 28507-3 $1.00

SELECTED POEMS, Walt Whitman. 128pp. 26878-0 $1.00

THE BALLAD OF READING GAOL AND OTHER POEMS, Oscar Wilde. 64pp. 27072-6 $1.00

EARLY POEMS, William Carlos Williams. 64pp. (Available in U.S. only.) 29294-0 $1.00

FAVORITE POEMS, William Wordsworth. 80pp. 27073-4 $1.00

WORLD WAR ONE BRITISH POETS: Brooke, Owen, Sassoon, Rosenberg, and Others, Candace Ward (ed.). (Available in U.S. only.) 29568-0 $1.00

EARLY POEMS, William Butler Yeats. 128pp. 27808-5 $1.50

"EASTER, 1916" AND OTHER POEMS, William Butler Yeats. 80pp. (Available in U.S. only.) 29771-3 $1.00

DOVER·THRIFT·EDITIONS

FICTION

FLATLAND: A ROMANCE OF MANY DIMENSIONS, Edwin A. Abbott. 96pp. 27263-X $1.00

SHORT STORIES, Louisa May Alcott. 64pp. 29063-8 $1.00

WINESBURG, OHIO, Sherwood Anderson. 160pp. 28269-4 $2.00

PERSUASION, Jane Austen. 224pp. 29555-9 $2.00

PRIDE AND PREJUDICE, Jane Austen. 272pp. 28473-5 $2.00

SENSE AND SENSIBILITY, Jane Austen. 272pp. 29049-2 $2.00

LOOKING BACKWARD, Edward Bellamy. 160pp. 29038-7 $2.00

BEOWULF, Beowulf (trans. by R. K. Gordon). 64pp. 27264-8 $1.00

CIVIL WAR STORIES, Ambrose Bierce. 128pp. 28038-1 $1.00

"THE MOONLIT ROAD" AND OTHER GHOST AND HORROR STORIES, Ambrose Bierce (John Grafton, ed.) 96pp. 40056-5 $1.00

WUTHERING HEIGHTS, Emily Brontë. 256pp. 29256-8 $2.00

THE THIRTY-NINE STEPS, John Buchan. 96pp. 28201-5 $1.50

TARZAN OF THE APES, Edgar Rice Burroughs. 224pp. (Available in U.S. only.) 29570-2 $2.00

ALICE'S ADVENTURES IN WONDERLAND, Lewis Carroll. 96pp. 27543-4 $1.00

THROUGH THE LOOKING-GLASS, Lewis Carroll. 128pp. 40878-7 $1.50

MY ÁNTONIA, Willa Cather. 176pp. 28240-6 $2.00

O PIONEERS!, Willa Cather. 128pp. 27785-2 $1.00

PAUL'S CASE AND OTHER STORIES, Willa Cather. 64pp. 29057-3 $1.00

FIVE GREAT SHORT STORIES, Anton Chekhov. 96pp. 26463-7 $1.00

TALES OF CONJURE AND THE COLOR LINE, Charles Waddell Chesnutt. 128pp. 40426-9 $1.50

FAVORITE FATHER BROWN STORIES, G. K. Chesterton. 96pp. 27545-0 $1.00

THE AWAKENING, Kate Chopin. 128pp. 27786-0 $1.00

A PAIR OF SILK STOCKINGS AND OTHER STORIES, Kate Chopin. 64pp. 29264-9 $1.00

HEART OF DARKNESS, Joseph Conrad. 80pp. 26464-5 $1.00

LORD JIM, Joseph Conrad. 256pp. 40650-4 $2.00

THE SECRET SHARER AND OTHER STORIES, Joseph Conrad. 128pp. 27546-9 $1.00

THE "LITTLE REGIMENT" AND OTHER CIVIL WAR STORIES, Stephen Crane. 80pp. 29557-5 $1.00

THE OPEN BOAT AND OTHER STORIES, Stephen Crane. 128pp. 27547-7 $1.50

THE RED BADGE OF COURAGE, Stephen Crane. 112pp. 26465-3 $1.00

MOLL FLANDERS, Daniel Defoe. 256pp. 29093-X $2.00

ROBINSON CRUSOE, Daniel Defoe. 288pp. 40427-7 $2.00

A CHRISTMAS CAROL, Charles Dickens. 80pp. 26865-9 $1.00

THE CRICKET ON THE HEARTH AND OTHER CHRISTMAS STORIES, Charles Dickens. 128pp. 28039-X $1.00

A TALE OF TWO CITIES, Charles Dickens. 304pp. 40651-2 $2.00

THE DOUBLE, Fyodor Dostoyevsky. 128pp. 29572-9 $1.50

THE GAMBLER, Fyodor Dostoyevsky. 112pp. 29081-6 $1.50

NOTES FROM THE UNDERGROUND, Fyodor Dostoyevsky. 96pp. 27053-X $1.00

THE ADVENTURE OF THE DANCING MEN AND OTHER STORIES, Sir Arthur Conan Doyle. 80pp. 29558-3 $1.00

THE HOUND OF THE BASKERVILLES, Arthur Conan Doyle. 128pp. 28214-7 $1.50

THE LOST WORLD, Arthur Conan Doyle. 176pp. 40060-3 $1.50

DOVER · THRIFT · EDITIONS

FICTION

SIX GREAT SHERLOCK HOLMES STORIES, Sir Arthur Conan Doyle. 112pp. 27055-6 $1.00

SILAS MARNER, George Eliot. 160pp. 29246-0 $1.50

THIS SIDE OF PARADISE, F. Scott Fitzgerald. 208pp. 28999-0 $2.00

"THE DIAMOND AS BIG AS THE RITZ" AND OTHER STORIES, F. Scott Fitzgerald. 29991-0 $2.00

THE REVOLT OF "MOTHER" AND OTHER STORIES, Mary E. Wilkins Freeman. 128pp. 40428-5 $1.50

MADAME BOVARY, Gustave Flaubert. 256pp. 29257-6 $2.00

WHERE ANGELS FEAR TO TREAD, E. M. Forster. 128pp. (Available in U.S. only.) 27791-7 $1.50

A ROOM WITH A VIEW, E. M. Forster. 176pp. (Available in U.S. only.) 28467-0 $2.00

THE IMMORALIST, André Gide. 112pp. (Available in U.S. only.) 29237-1 $1.50

"THE YELLOW WALLPAPER" AND OTHER STORIES, Charlotte Perkins Gilman. 80pp. 29857-4 $1.00

HERLAND, Charlotte Perkins Gilman. 128pp. 40429-3 $1.50

THE OVERCOAT AND OTHER STORIES, Nikolai Gogol. 112pp. 27057-2 $1.50

GREAT GHOST STORIES, John Grafton (ed.). 112pp. 27270-2 $1.00

DETECTION BY GASLIGHT, Douglas G. Greene (ed.). 272pp. 29928-7 $2.00

THE MABINOGION, Lady Charlotte E. Guest. 192pp. 29541-9 $2.00

"THE FIDDLER OF THE REELS" AND OTHER SHORT STORIES, Thomas Hardy. 80pp. 29960-0 $1.50

THE LUCK OF ROARING CAMP AND OTHER STORIES, Bret Harte. 96pp. 27271-0 $1.00

THE SCARLET LETTER, Nathaniel Hawthorne. 192pp. 28048-9 $2.00

YOUNG GOODMAN BROWN AND OTHER STORIES, Nathaniel Hawthorne. 128pp. 27060-2 $1.00

THE GIFT OF THE MAGI AND OTHER SHORT STORIES, O. Henry. 96pp. 27061-0 $1.00

THE NUTCRACKER AND THE GOLDEN POT, E. T. A. Hoffmann. 128pp. 27806-9 $1.00

THE BEAST IN THE JUNGLE AND OTHER STORIES, Henry James. 128pp. 27552-3 $1.50

DAISY MILLER, Henry James. 64pp. 28773-4 $1.00

THE TURN OF THE SCREW, Henry James. 96pp. 26684-2 $1.00

WASHINGTON SQUARE, Henry James. 176pp. 40431-5 $2.00

THE COUNTRY OF THE POINTED FIRS, Sarah Orne Jewett. 96pp. 28196-5 $1.00

THE AUTOBIOGRAPHY OF AN EX-COLORED MAN, James Weldon Johnson. 112pp. 28512-X $1.00

DUBLINERS, James Joyce. 160pp. 26870-5 $1.00

A PORTRAIT OF THE ARTIST AS A YOUNG MAN, James Joyce. 192pp. 28050-0 $2.00

THE METAMORPHOSIS AND OTHER STORIES, Franz Kafka. 96pp. 29030-1 $1.50

THE MAN WHO WOULD BE KING AND OTHER STORIES, Rudyard Kipling. 128pp. 28051-9 $1.50

YOU KNOW ME AL, Ring Lardner. 128pp. 28513-8 $1.50

SELECTED SHORT STORIES, D. H. Lawrence. 128pp. 27794-1 $1.50

GREEN TEA AND OTHER GHOST STORIES, J. Sheridan LeFanu. 96pp. 27795-X $1.50

SHORT STORIES, Theodore Dreiser. 112pp. 28215-5 $1.50

THE CALL OF THE WILD, Jack London. 64pp. 26472-6 $1.00

FIVE GREAT SHORT STORIES, Jack London. 96pp. 27063-7 $1.00

WHITE FANG, Jack London. 160pp. 26968-X $1.00

DEATH IN VENICE, Thomas Mann. 96pp. (Available in U.S. only.) 28714-9 $1.00

IN A GERMAN PENSION: 13 Stories, Katherine Mansfield. 112pp. 28719-X $1.50

THE MOON AND SIXPENCE, W. Somerset Maugham. 176pp. (Available in U.S. only.) 28731-9 $2.00

DOVER · THRIFT · EDITIONS

FICTION

THE NECKLACE AND OTHER SHORT STORIES, Guy de Maupassant. 128pp. 27064-5 $1.00

BARTLEBY AND BENITO CERENO, Herman Melville. 112pp. 26473-4 $1.00

THE OIL JAR AND OTHER STORIES, Luigi Pirandello. 96pp. 28459-X $1.00

THE GOLD-BUG AND OTHER TALES, Edgar Allan Poe. 128pp. 26875-6 $1.00

TALES OF TERROR AND DETECTION, Edgar Allan Poe. 96pp. 28744-0 $1.00

THE QUEEN OF SPADES AND OTHER STORIES, Alexander Pushkin. 128pp. 28054-3 $1.50

SREDNI VASHTAR AND OTHER STORIES, Saki (H. H. Munro). 96pp. 28521-9 $1.00

THE STORY OF AN AFRICAN FARM, Olive Schreiner. 256pp. 40165-0 $2.00

FRANKENSTEIN, Mary Shelley. 176pp. 28211-2 $1.00

THREE LIVES, Gertrude Stein. 176pp. (Available in U.S. only.) 28059-4 $2.00

THE STRANGE CASE OF DR. JEKYLL AND MR. HYDE, Robert Louis Stevenson. 64pp. 26688-5 $1.00

TREASURE ISLAND, Robert Louis Stevenson. 160pp. 27559-0 $1.50

GULLIVER'S TRAVELS, Jonathan Swift. 240pp. 29273-8 $2.00

THE KREUTZER SONATA AND OTHER SHORT STORIES, Leo Tolstoy. 144pp. 27805-0 $1.50

THE WARDEN, Anthony Trollope. 176pp. 40076-X $2.00

FIRST LOVE AND DIARY OF A SUPERFLUOUS MAN, Ivan Turgenev. 96pp. 28775-0 $1.50

FATHERS AND SONS, Ivan Turgenev. 176pp. 40073-5 $2.00

ADVENTURES OF HUCKLEBERRY FINN, Mark Twain. 224pp. 28061-6 $2.00

THE ADVENTURES OF TOM SAWYER, Mark Twain. 192pp. 40077-8 $2.00

THE MYSTERIOUS STRANGER AND OTHER STORIES, Mark Twain. 128pp. 27069-6 $1.00

HUMOROUS STORIES AND SKETCHES, Mark Twain. 80pp. 29279-7 $1.00

CANDIDE, Voltaire (François-Marie Arouet). 112pp. 26689-3 $1.00

GREAT SHORT STORIES BY AMERICAN WOMEN, Candace Ward (ed.). 192pp. 28776-9 $2.00

"THE COUNTRY OF THE BLIND" AND OTHER SCIENCE-FICTION STORIES, H. G. Wells. 160pp. (Available in U.S. only.) 29569-9 $1.00

THE ISLAND OF DR. MOREAU, H. G. Wells. 112pp. (Available in U.S. only.) 29027-1 $1.50

THE INVISIBLE MAN, H. G. Wells. 112pp. (Available in U.S. only.) 27071-8 $1.00

THE TIME MACHINE, H. G. Wells. 80pp. (Available in U.S. only.) 28472-7 $1.00

THE WAR OF THE WORLDS, H. G. Wells. 160pp. (Available in U.S. only.) 29506-0 $1.00

ETHAN FROME, Edith Wharton. 96pp. 26690-7 $1.00

SHORT STORIES, Edith Wharton. 128pp. 28235-X $1.50

THE AGE OF INNOCENCE, Edith Wharton. 288pp. 29803-5 $2.00

THE PICTURE OF DORIAN GRAY, Oscar Wilde. 192pp. 27807-7 $1.50

JACOB'S ROOM, Virginia Woolf. 144pp. (Available in U.S. only.) 40109-X $1.50

MONDAY OR TUESDAY: Eight Stories, Virginia Woolf. 64pp. (Available in U.S. only.) 29453-6 $1.00

NONFICTION

POETICS, Aristotle. 64pp. 29577-X $1.00

NICOMACHEAN ETHICS, Aristotle. 256pp. 40096-4 $2.00

MEDITATIONS, Marcus Aurelius. 128pp. 29823-X $1.50

THE LAND OF LITTLE RAIN, Mary Austin. 96pp. 29037-9 $1.50

THE DEVIL'S DICTIONARY, Ambrose Bierce. 144pp. 27542-6 $1.00

THE ANALECTS, Confucius. 128pp. 28484-0 $2.00

CONFESSIONS OF AN ENGLISH OPIUM EATER, Thomas De Quincey. 80pp. 28742-4 $1.00

NARRATIVE OF THE LIFE OF FREDERICK DOUGLASS, Frederick Douglass. 96pp. 28499-9 $1.00

DOVER·THRIFT·EDITIONS

NONFICTION

THE SOULS OF BLACK FOLK, W. E. B. Du Bois. 176pp. 28041-1 $2.00

SELF-RELIANCE AND OTHER ESSAYS, Ralph Waldo Emerson. 128pp. 27790-9 $1.00

THE LIFE OF OLAUDAH EQUIANO, OR GUSTAVUS VASSA, THE AFRICAN, Olaudah Equiano. 192pp. 40661-X $2.00

THE AUTOBIOGRAPHY OF BENJAMIN FRANKLIN, Benjamin Franklin. 144pp. 29073-5 $1.50

TOTEM AND TABOO, Sigmund Freud. 176pp. (Available in U.S. only.) 40434-X $2.00

LOVE: A Book of Quotations, Herb Galewitz (ed.). 64pp. 40004-2 $1.00

PRAGMATISM, William James. 128pp. 28270-8 $1.50

THE STORY OF MY LIFE, Helen Keller. 80pp. 29249-5 $1.00

TAO TE CHING, Lao Tze. 112pp. 29792-6 $1.00

GREAT SPEECHES, Abraham Lincoln. 112pp. 26872-1 $1.00

THE PRINCE, Niccolò Machiavelli. 80pp. 27274-5 $1.00

THE SUBJECTION OF WOMEN, John Stuart Mill. 112pp. 29601-6 $1.50

SELECTED ESSAYS, Michel de Montaigne. 96pp. 29109-X $1.50

UTOPIA, Sir Thomas More. 96pp. 29583-4 $1.50

BEYOND GOOD AND EVIL: Prelude to a Philosophy of the Future, Friedrich Nietzsche. 176pp. 29868-X $1.50

THE BIRTH OF TRAGEDY, Friedrich Nietzsche. 96pp. 28515-4 $1.50

COMMON SENSE, Thomas Paine. 64pp. 29602-4 $1.00

SYMPOSIUM AND PHAEDRUS, Plato. 96pp. 27798-4 $1.50

THE TRIAL AND DEATH OF SOCRATES: Four Dialogues, Plato. 128pp. 27066-1 $1.00

A MODEST PROPOSAL AND OTHER SATIRICAL WORKS, Jonathan Swift. 64pp. 28759-9 $1.00

CIVIL DISOBEDIENCE AND OTHER ESSAYS, Henry David Thoreau. 96pp. 27563-9 $1.00

SELECTIONS FROM THE JOURNALS (Edited by Walter Harding), Henry David Thoreau. 96pp. 28760-2 $1.00

WALDEN; OR, LIFE IN THE WOODS, Henry David Thoreau. 224pp. 28495-6 $2.00

NARRATIVE OF SOJOURNER TRUTH, Sojourner Truth. 80pp. 29899-X $1.00

THE THEORY OF THE LEISURE CLASS, Thorstein Veblen. 256pp. 28062-4 $2.50

DE PROFUNDIS, Oscar Wilde. 64pp. 29308-4 $1.00

OSCAR WILDE'S WIT AND WISDOM: A Book of Quotations, Oscar Wilde. 64pp. 40146-4 $1.00

UP FROM SLAVERY, Booker T. Washington. 160pp. 28738-6 $2.00

A VINDICATION OF THE RIGHTS OF WOMAN, Mary Wollstonecraft. 224pp. 29036-0 $2.00

PLAYS

PROMETHEUS BOUND, Aeschylus. 64pp. 28762-9 $1.00

THE ORESTEIA TRILOGY: Agamemnon, The Libation-Bearers and The Furies, Aeschylus. 160pp. 29242-8 $1.50

LYSISTRATA, Aristophanes. 64pp. 28225-2 $1.00

WHAT EVERY WOMAN KNOWS, James Barrie. 80pp. (Available in U.S. only.) 29578-8 $1.50

THE CHERRY ORCHARD, Anton Chekhov. 64pp. 26682-6 $1.00

THE SEA GULL, Anton Chekhov. 64pp. 40656-3 $1.50

THE THREE SISTERS, Anton Chekhov. 64pp. 27544-2 $1.50

UNCLE VANYA, Anton Chekhov. 64pp. 40159-6 $1.50

THE WAY OF THE WORLD, William Congreve. 80pp. 27787-9 $1.50

BACCHAE, Euripides. 64pp. 29580-X $1.00

MEDEA, Euripides. 64pp. 27548-5 $1.00

THE MIKADO, William Schwenck Gilbert. 64pp. 27268-0 $1.50